BOARDROOM SECRETS

BOARDROOM SECRETS

CORPORATE GOVERNANCE FOR QUALITY OF LIFE

Yılmaz Argüden

Chairman, ARGE Consulting
Chairman, Rothschild, Turkey

palgrave
macmillan

First published in English in 2009 by
PALGRAVE MACMILLAN

Palgrave Macmillan in the UK is an imprint of Macmillan Publishers Limited, registered in England, company number 785998, of Houndmills, Basingstoke, Hampshire' RG21 6XS.

Palgrave Macmillan in the US is a division of St Martin's Press LLC, 175 Fifth Avenue, New York, NY 10010.

Palgrave Macmillan is the global academic imprint of the above companies and has companies and representatives throughout the world.

Palgrave® and Macmillan® are registered trademarks in the United States, the United Kingdom, Europe and other countries

ISBN 978–0–230–23077–4

This book is printed on paper suitable for recycling and made from fully managed and sustained forest sources. Logging, pulping and manufacturing processes are expected to conform to the environmental regulations of the country of origin.

A catalogue record for this book is available from the British Library.

A catalog record for this book is available from the Library of Congress.

10 9 8 7 6 5 4 3 2 1
18 17 16 15 14 13 12 11 10 09

Printed and bound in Great Britain by
CPI Antony Rowe, Chippenham and Eastbourne

Dedication

To my father, who taught me the value of ethical conduct and self-discipline ...

To my mother, who taught me positive and constructive thinking and pre-emptive planning ...

To my wife, who brought color and peace of mind to my life ...

And to my children, in whom my hopes for the future flourish ...

Contents

Preface

Trust is the foundation of development both in relations among humans, as well as in relations between institutions such as the firm and its stakeholders. As the world continues to get smaller, the mutual interdependence of the corporations and their stakeholders grows larger. To achieve success, institutions rely increasingly upon the utilization of not only their own resources, but also those of others. In order to gain access to the resources of others, institutions need to create trustworthy relationships. Therefore, the key to success and development is gaining the trust of present and potential stakeholders.

For example, in order to be able to grow fast and compete globally firms need to gain access to global credit or equity capital markets. Similarly, as the role of corporations in the development of the world's economy increases and the scope of their influence widens, so does the breadth of their responsibilities. License to operate increasingly requires fulfillment of the firms' responsibilities toward the community. The trustworthiness of corporate architectures, processes, and behaviors becomes an indispensable characteristic of the corporation not only for their shareholders, but also for their stakeholders and in particular for financial markets. The quality of management is a function of the competencies of the people, as well as the organizational infrastructure and culture.

Corporate governance refers to the reliability and transparency of the organizational infrastructure that defines not only the principles of the relations between the large and small shareholders, the board of directors, the top management, and the employees, but also the way responsibilities and authority are distributed throughout the organization. The relevance of corporate governance is not limited to the aforementioned groups, but extends further to creditors, suppliers, customers, and society as a whole. Corporate governance is the foundation of corporate trust.

While there is no single recipe for corporate trust, certain applications are considered good practice. For example, the principle of the separation of powers, a key principle in democracies, is applied to corporations by separating the roles of the chairperson and the CEO, or by making sure that the audit committees are comprised of independent members of the board, who are also responsible for the hiring and oversight of the independent audit firms.

One of the key elements of gaining trust is transparency. For this reason, the timely, simultaneous, and adequate disclosure of relevant information to all stakeholders is increasingly becoming the norm for gaining trust. In corporate disclosures, being fair to all stakeholders, and not differentiating among the shareholders, regardless of the size of their holdings or whether if they are represented on the board, is a key requirement. Hence we see the increasing prevalence of insider-trading restrictions and strict disclosure requirements, especially for public companies.

Gaining the trust of others is a valuable but difficult endeavor, not only for individuals, but also for institutions. While achieving the status of being trustworthy is a long process, trust could be lost very quickly. In gaining trust, actions speak louder than words, as consistency of actions is a more dependable indicator of preferences and priorities than words.

Corporations that flourish through the utilization of global resources are becoming increasingly aware of the need to be accountable towards those who have a stake in those resources. As our dependence on global resources increases, we need to be aware of the need to have our governance systems and attitudes gain a global dimension as well. Throughout the world, religions are notable for their longevity as institutions. The level of transparency and accountability that is being faced by the corporations seeking longevity parallels some key principles of religions, such as assuming responsibility for one's actions regardless of the existence of a witness; or the impossibility of escaping from the day of reckoning.

Today, successful and sustainable organizations need to demonstrate a willingness to involve stakeholders in decision-making; to embrace a culture of transparency and accountability; to be fair and consistent in relations with stakeholders; and to have an organizational infrastructure that ensures "corporate trust."

The most important element of organizational infrastructure is the board of directors. The board has the ultimate decision-making power and therefore the ultimate responsibility towards the stakeholders and the sustainability of the corporation. Therefore, issues such as the composition, the agenda, the processes of the board, and how the board develops its own effectiveness as a team are key to ensuring the quality of the governance of a corporation. Quality of governance is as dependent on the organizational structure and decision-making processes of the firm as it is on the quality of the key people that make up the board and the management team.

The board does not run the company. Rather, they guide and advise the management, veto decisions that they deem inappropriate, and make changes to the management team if and when they see fit. The board's responsibility is providing guidance and oversight to the management in order to ensure that the company creates value on a sustainable basis while protecting the interests of all stakeholders. The essence of good corporate governance is ensuring trustworthy relations between the corporation and its stakeholders.

Boards have received the blame for recent notable corporate failures. This has caused numerous initiatives to establish strict guidelines for governance, such as the Sarbanes–Oxley Act. Furthermore, with the perspectives of the audit firms and legal advisors, compliance issues have gained more importance. While rules and regulations are important, it would be naive to assume that good governance can be achieved only through regulation.

Governance is much more than compliance. Good corporate governance is a culture and a climate of consistency, responsibility, accountability, fairness, transparency, and effectiveness that is deployed throughout the organization. The purpose of this book is to improve the understanding of the spirit, principles, and behavioral aspects of good corporate governance. I wish to provide clues to improving the quality of governance in every kind of corporation, in different industries, of differing sizes, and of differing shareholding structures because the same fundamentals apply to them all.

Ten years ago when we initiated the National Quality Movement (NQM) in Turkey to introduce total quality management to all kinds of organizations, small or large, public or private, located throughout the country, it was deemed to be an unachievable dream as there was the preconceived notion that the philosophy of quality pertained only to large, exporter, private sector establishments. Today, in 10 short years thanks to the NQM, we have observed that small and large, private and public sector corporations, and even NGOs, hospitals, and schools, are adopting the quality philosophy. This pioneering effort led to Turkey being consistently one of the top two countries in winning European Quality Awards and last year a public sector hospital from an Anatolian town won the European Quality Award.

I wish to emphasize that the key principles and lessons outlined in this book are equally universal. They apply to all kinds of corporations, regardless of size, industry, shareholding structure, or jurisdiction. This book attempts to go beyond the veil of compliance issues to uncover the fundamental understanding and behaviors required for the sustainable network of relations that each corporation needs for survival. In doing so, I hope to be able to contribute to a world where the governance and management quality of our institutions are continuously improved.

I could not have gained the understanding of governance that I wish to share through this book without the opportunity to work with hundreds of colleagues in many institutions across the globe. I hold them in the highest esteem and thank each and every one of them for their invaluable contributions towards the development of my ideas on this subject matter. I would also like to thank the colleagues with whom I have had the pleasure to serve on boards of numerous organizations. I am also grateful to my teachers throughout my academic life, who have instilled the importance of sharing knowledge, and to my colleagues at ARGE Consulting, especially Pınar Ilgaz and Burak Erşahin, who have helped enrich the ideas set forth in this book.

Additionally, many thanks are due to Aclan Acar from Doğş Holding, Agah Uğur from Borusan, Alev Yaraman from Şişe Cam, former Undersecretary of the State Planning Organization Ali Tiğrel, former Chairman of the Turkish Airlines Cem Kozlu, former President of Durable Consumer Goods at the Koç Group Cengiz Solakoğlu, Ege Cansen from the Anadolu Group, former Chairman of the Turkish Industrialists' and Businessmen's Association Erkut Yücaoğlu, Hasan Subaşı from the Koç Holding, the intellectual architect of the new Turkish Commercial Code Ünal Tekinalp, respected banking executive Vural Akışık, and from the Corporate Governance Association of Turkey, Güray Karacar, Eser Özer and former President Ümit Hergüner, for their contributions and suggestions on the first draft of this book. Last, but not least, I would like to extend my sincere thanks to Keith Povey and Mark Henry for their excellent editorial help, Eleanor Davey Corrigan for her meticulous efforts to get the book ready for publication, Stephen Rutt, Global Publishing Director at Palgrave Macmillan, for his enduring support, and my son Ege for his contribution to cover design.

It is my sincere wish that this book will be useful in the development of corporate governance culture, and contributes to the establishment of trustworthy relationships between corporations and their stakeholders, thereby ensuring effective, sustainable, and equitable resource utilization to improve the quality of life throughout the globe.

YILMAZ ARGÜDEN

Introduction: Why Corporate Governance?

Trust is the foundation of sustainable success. Companies who earn the trust of their stakeholders are able to mobilize more resources throughout their value chain to achieve sustainable success. The essence of good corporate governance is ensuring trustworthy relations between the corporation and its stakeholders. This is the fundamental reason why good corporate governance is being embraced by companies in diverse industries, small and large, publicly or privately owned, throughout the world.

Good corporate governance is the key to attracting financial and human capital to the corporation and strong business partners to the value chain, and to ensuring sustainability of value creation. Corporate governance refers to the quality, transparency, and dependability of the relationships between the shareholders, board of directors, management, and employees that define the authority and responsibility of each in delivering sustainable value to all the stakeholders.

While good governance is the responsibility of all those who conduct relations with the stakeholders, it is the board of directors who sets the tone at the top and are responsible for ensuring that the right climate and culture exist within the organization. The key to good corporate governance is ensuring that the principles of Consistency, Responsibility, Accountability, Fairness, Transparency, and Effectiveness are Deployed (CRAFTED) throughout the organization. Applying CRAFTED principles is a *sine qua non* of sustainable success. Any lapse in applying these principles results in the failure of even global giants such as like Enron, Arthur Anderson, or more recent notable corporate casualties, at the blink of an eye.

Earning the trust of the stakeholders is the key to mobilizing their resources towards a common vision. Transparency in the relationships is the key to earning that trust. Success requires effective utilization of resources entrusted to a corporation. Being fair and accountable to all the stakeholders whose resources are entrusted to the corporation is the key to the sustainability of access to those resources. The communication and behavior of each institution influences not only how its own resources are utilized, but also those of its stakeholders. Therefore, consistency of the policies of a corporation is the key to ensuring that the right expectations are formed throughout the value chain, thereby making the whole value chain stronger. Value creation requires measured risk-taking. Risk is the kin of profit. Therefore, taking initiative and responsibility which naturally involves risk-taking is a key element of value creation. Sustainability of success requires continuous improvement and innovation. This in turn requires the participation and involvement of all in the organization. Hence, creation of a climate that emphasizes good governance principles and deployment of a good corporate governance culture is the key to sustainability.

Executives are responsible for managing a corporation on behalf of its shareholders. In order to ensure that the risks taken by management on behalf of the shareholders are consistent and balanced, and to prevent any potential conflicts of interest between the management and shareholders, effective guidance and oversight are required. Provision of such guidance and oversight requires an in-depth knowledge of the industry dynamics and the company's competitive positioning. The sustainability of an organization requires striking a fine balance between risk and reward, and ensuring that there are effective internal control mechanisms. This in turn requires a fair process to challenge the management about their decisions, particularly on strategic choices. The board of directors is the key to providing such guidance and oversight. The relevance of the experience and expertise of the board members to the corporation's business and risk profile, their integrity, independence, involvement, and their understanding of fiduciary duties, are critical for ensuring the sustainability of the corporation.

Among the most important assets of a corporation are its human resources, especially its management team. The competencies and performance of this team must be assessed and new members introduced should the need arise. Another factor that will determine the future of a corporation is the introduction of a fair reward mechanism designed to maintain a high level of motivation among team members. A board that operates soundly will ensure that these assessments are conducted in a fair and balanced manner.

The mission of the board, as the highest decision-making authority, is to guide the corporation in a proactive manner and, in the long term, to ensure that value is created for its shareholders. One of the most important elements that pave the road to success is the corporate strategy. The essence of strategy is choice. Therefore, each strategic choice entails risk, because making one decision means rejecting another. Taking one road means eliminating another. Strategic choices are intended for the future, whereas the future is uncertain. The quality of strategic decisions can be enhanced by boards that scrutinize these strategic choices based on the experience of their members. Therefore, having a board with sufficiently diverse experience, and critical and independent thinking skills to challenge the strategic choices from multiple perspectives increases the probability of success.

The fiduciary duties of the board require them to oversee the protection of corporate assets, tangible as well as intangible. For example, protection of the reputation of the corporation in the minds of all its stakeholders requires board oversight, not only from a financial or legal perspective but also with respect to value creation capabilities.

Therefore, the composition, processes, and culture of the board of directors are critical for the sustainability of the organization. Adherence to good corporate governance principles is a precursor to continuously improving management quality. In many countries where families hold controlling stakes in the corporations, the relationship between the board and the majority partner is often the greatest obstacle to the development of corporate governance. For this reason, a critical priority for the board of directors is to assume responsibility for the guidance and oversight of the corporation rather than implicitly assuming the role of an advisor to the controlling shareholder. Boards are responsible not only for looking out for the interests of an institution's largest shareholder but also for overseeing the interests of other small shareholders and all stakeholders alike.[1]

The board of directors is among the most important strategic assets of any institution. Consequently, the competencies and experience of the board members, and their ability to remain independent and to adhere to the principles of good governance, bear great importance on the institution's success and sustainability.

Corporate governance is relevant not only for large publicly traded companies, but also for SMEs, for family businesses, and even for non-profit organizations, as each of these organizations is dependent on sustainable access to the resources of other stakeholders, and would benefit from balanced guidance and oversight. Therefore, having a reputable board may be useful in avoiding family conflicts, in attracting talent, and in improving the reputation and value of the organization. A good board can also aid in attracting partners, in raising capital and in supporting the establishment of trustworthy partnerships with the stakeholders.

In order to be competitive, organizations should apply good governance principles. This is not due to some external pressure such as that from the OECD, EU, World Bank, IMF, shareholder activist, or any regulatory agency, but in order to ensure proper management of risks, to be more competitive, and to gain access to more resources for continuous development.

NOTE

1 In some jurisdictions, such as the United States, the main responsibility of the board members is defined as protecting the interests of shareholders; in other jurisdictions, such as Canada, directors' duties require them to consider carefully the reasonable expectations of all stakeholders (see the decision dated December 2008 of the Supreme Court of Canada on the BCE case). The Dutch Corporate Governance Code also assigns the responsibility for reasonable and fair dealing with all stakeholders to the board. The author is of the view that for sustainable success a corporation as an ongoing concern needs to balance the expectations of all of its stakeholders.

CHAPTER 1

Right People

Pearls are not found in shallow waters.
If you want one, you must dive deep in order to uncover it.

Chinese proverb

COMPETENCIES OF BOARD MEMBERS

The key to a successfully functioning board is the character and competencies of the people who make up that board. While the character requirements may be common, the competency requirements may vary depending on the issues facing the company. Nevertheless, there are some key competencies that are *sine qua nons* for board membership. As the board members have the fiduciary responsibility **to guide** and **to provide oversight** to the company as an ongoing concern, they have to not only protect the company, but also to ensure value creation for the stakeholders on a sustainable basis. They have **to exercise judgment on** such **critical dimensions** as risk vs. reward, short-term vs. long-term interests, effective oversight vs. motivating management, ethical considerations vs. market practices in different jurisdictions, and balancing the competing interests of different stakeholders.

In order for anyone to be qualified as a board member he/she therefore has to have a proven track record that demonstrates integrity and high ethical standards; financial literacy; an understanding of fiduciary duty; well-developed listening, communicating, and influencing skills, so that every individual director can proactively participate in board discussions and debate; and expertise relevant to the corporation's business purpose, financial responsibilities, and risk profile. In addition, each has to be able to devote sufficient time and attention to assume the responsibilities of serving as a director.

Because board decisions require complex evaluations in multiple dimensions, bringing different views to the table and having the opportunity to evaluate different perspectives provides an opportunity for better judgment. Therefore, the board members' independence, impartiality, and self-confidence in challenging issues from different perspectives are critically valuable characteristics. Especially when there is a strong chairperson and/or CEO in the boardroom, the ability and propensity to challenge decisions requires a high degree of self-confidence, as well as the relevant experience to support it. The ability to say "no" when necessary is a critical test of independence. However, it should be clear that the role of the board members is not to paralyze decision-making by always raising concerns on numerous aspects, but rather to ensure that every aspect of a decision is considered, the necessary precautions taken, and the decisions are reached in a timely manner.

In order for the members of the board to conduct their tasks in an efficient manner, they should have **experience in various areas** such as strategy, finance, law, and technology, in addition to a **special focus** on **the future and sustainability** of the company. At the same time, a **holistic outlook** and **prudent judgment** are keys to a successful board.

The basic criterion to be applied when choosing members is the value that they will add to the board. Aside from being knowledgeable and experienced, this value can be generated from being able to share opinions with their fellow board members and the management freely, openly, and in a constructive manner.

If everybody thinks the same on all matters, then there is no need for a board. One individual would suffice! Therefore, in order to bring diversity of opinion to the board, experience from different industries is valuable. For example, the board members of Nestlé do not come solely from the food industry (see Table 1.1). Members of the Nestlé board have experience in different industries and are able to address issues that are important to Nestlé, such as: following the new trends closely (for example, politics and academia), understanding the needs of youth (for example, technology, multimedia), understanding capital and credit markets (for example, banking and finance), and focusing on health and beauty (for example, pharmaceutical, cosmetics). Although the board members come from different fields, they all have senior management experience and possess the skills to guide and to provide oversight to the company.

The attributes sought in board members can be classified into two categories. The first come under general characteristics that must be present in all members; the second are those competencies that are sought on an individual basis, whose possessors provide diversity and different areas of expertise as members of a team. Common attributes stem from the basic role and duties of the board, while individually required competencies are required to provide both diversity and a good coverage of the issues facing the company.

Table 1.1 Nestlé Board of Directors 2007

1.	Peter Brabeck-Latmanthe	Chairman and CEO, Nestlé	
2.	Adreas Koopmann	CEO, Bobst Group	Packaging (cartons etc.)
3.	Rolf Hanggi	Deputy Chairman, Roche	Pharmaceutical
4.	Edward George	Former Member, Bank of England	Finance
5.	Kaspar Villiger	Former Minister, Switzerland	Politics
6.	Jean-Pierre Meyers	Deputy Chairman, L'Oreal	Cosmetics
7.	Peter Böckli	Attorney	Legal
8.	Andre Kudelski	Chairman and CEO, Kudelski Group	Technology (Digital Safety)
9.	Daniel Borel	Chairman, Logitech	Technology (Computers etc.)
10.	Carolina Müller-Möhl	Chairman, Müller-Möhl Group	Asset Management
11.	Günter Bobel	Professor, Rockefeller University	Academician
12.	Jean-Rene Fourtou	Chairman, Vivendi Universal	Multimedia (TV, music, etc.)
13.	Steven George Hoch	Partner, Highmount Capital	Finance (Investment Management)
14.	Niana Lal Kidwai	CEO, HSBC India	Finance

Common Attributes of Board Members

- Knowledge and experience to understand and lead an organization, understanding all aspects of stakeholder management.
- Integrity and high ethical standards.
- Conformity with the corporation's values.
- Understanding of fiduciary responsibility.
- Financial literacy.
- Ability to make judgments on decisions with implications in numerous dimensions.
- Independent thinking and the ability to express thoughts in a constructive manner.
- Exhibiting a constructive approach that is conducive to teamwork.
- Having internalized the principles of corporate governance.
- Believing in and applying standards of stretch performance.

- Being prepared to devote sufficient time and attention to be sufficiently informed and involved to assume the responsibilities to serve as a director.

- Willingness to take initiative to be proactive, challenge the management, and when needed take action.

Individually Required Competencies of Board Members

- **Sector experience** Leadership, national and international knowledge, and experience within industries that may have relevance to the corporation,

- **Stakeholder experience** Understanding the concerns and inner workings of key stakeholders for the corporation, that will allow the board member to guide the corporation both during the process of developing strategies and in implementing them.

- **Senior management experience** Possession of skills and experience deep enough in certain functional areas to provide benchmarks, and wide enough to understand the interrelationships between functions to guide the continuous development of management quality.

- **Senior-level relationships** Having strong, strategically important relationships with national and international institutions that are relevant for the corporation.

- **Geographic or issue-based experience** Having a good understanding of the trends and environment which are relevant to the corporation, or having experience relevant to the life cycle of the corporation. For example, if a firm is making a significant investment in a new geographical area, board members with the experience both in that geography and with the management of mega-projects would be beneficial.

THE POOL OF POTENTIAL BOARD MEMBERS

Traditionally, board members are picked by the largest shareholder, the chairperson, or the CEO. The personal connections of the largest shareholder or the CEO may in fact be useful in attracting valuable members to the board, but it also increases the risk of the board being comprised of "acquaintances" who may hesitate to challenge the CEO.

Also, not having a specific process to establish a wide enough pool of potential candidates may impede accomplished individuals joining the board and limit the diversity of the board's joint experience.

Each board must actively seek out skilled and competent individuals (candidates) and ensure that sufficient diversity of experience is brought to the boardroom. As it is difficult for the full board to conduct such a search, the corporate governance committee is generally charged with this duty. However, the final decision should be taken by the full board in the light of the committee's work. It may also be helpful to rely upon the expertise of specialists in this area when seeking out new independent members for the board.

The search process should employ an open-minded approach so as to reach a wide pool of candidates. Then each candidate should be evaluated for their competencies as a board member, their fit within the team, their potential contributions to the issues facing the company, and how they can enhance the diversity of that particular board. One other consideration must be the ability of a candidate to provide sufficient time and attention to that board. For example, a member who is a CEO at another corporation cannot normally be expected to take on more than two or three independent board membership positions.

Corporate Governance Principles (General Electric, 2007)

1. Selection of New Directors

The Board itself should be responsible, in fact as well as procedure, for selecting its own members and in recommending them for election by the stockholders. The Board delegates the screening process involved to the Directors and Corporate Governance Committee with direct input from the Chairman and Chief Executive Officer. The Directors and Corporate Governance Committee will consider director nominees recommended by stockholders. The Committee uses the same criteria for screening candidates proposed by stockholders, members of the Board, and members of senior management. Between annual stockholder meetings, the Board may elect Directors to serve until the next annual meeting.

2. Extending the Invitation to a Potential Director to Join the Board

The invitation to join the Board should be extended by the Board itself via the Chairman and Chief Executive Officer of the Corporation, together with an independent Director, when appropriate.

INDEPENDENT BOARD MEMBERS

Corporate governance codes becoming prevalent throughout the world are calling for the majority of any board to be comprised of independent members. A key mission for independent board members is to ensure that "the agency problem" between the shareholders and the management is handled in an equitable manner. This requires there to be proper evaluations of the risk–reward balance, of short-term vs. long-term returns, and of potential conflicts of interest. Another key requirement is the prevention of the preferential treatment of any stakeholder. Therefore, independent board members need to be not only competent but also sufficiently informed to make judgments to ensure the sustainability of the company. Furthermore, this is to be done not by taking over the role of the management, but rather in an indirect way by ensuring that the management of the company takes the necessary decisions and actions with this understanding.

The fundamental aim of governance codes is not compliance, but ensuring that the company is properly managed and that the interests

---

Who Is an Independent Board Member?
(Regulatory Definition)

- If the member is a shareholder, the shares must have been awarded through being a member of the board and may not exceed a total of 5%.

- The member must not have worked at the corporation, at any establishment tied to the corporation, at a sister company, or at any affiliate in the past 2 years.

- They must not be employed at any company that provides the corporation with a substantial service and product.

- They must not have any spouse or first-degree relative as an important shareholder in the corporation; at the corporation in any management capacity; or at a position to influence the internal control mechanisms of the corporation.

- If an individual is a shareholder because of their duty as a member of the board, their shares may not exceed the minority level defined by law, and their earnings must be within the limits of board membership remuneration and dividends on their minority holdings as a board member.

- They must not represent any large shareholder.

---

of shareholders in particular (but also the interests of all the stake-holders in order to ensure sustainability) are protected. Therefore, the key role of the independent board members is **to provide guidance** and **oversight** to ensure sustainable value creation. This is not only the individual responsibility of each member but also the joint respon-sibility of the board as a team.

In general, corporate governance codes define independence, as dis-cussed in the box, in terms of the financial interest of the member.

However, looking at the concept of independence only from a financial standpoint may not be sufficient. What is needed is a sound understanding of the reasoning underlying the independence criteria as well as the multiple perspectives of independence.

In some countries, "independence" is strictly defined as having no financial interest in the company other than the board membership fees. Such a definition not only makes it difficult to align the interests of board members and shareholders, but also is not necessarily in line with the spirit of independence. For example, had we been able to convince one of the best managers on the globe, say Jack Welch, to serve on the board of a corporation in such a jurisdiction, and had we organized a 2-day paid training session by Jack Welch for our managers, would this situation have affected the independence of his opinions while serving on the board? Would a person with an esti-mated fortune of hundreds of millions of dollars have been swayed in his judgment by being paid a consulting/training fee? Would forgoing such a training session, to remove any inkling of doubt, have been in the interests of the corporation? On the other hand, were we to appoint a retired civil servant as a member of our board, and were his/her salary three times that of his/her retirement pension, how would we, knowing that he/she had no other income, evaluate his/her standing with regard to financial independence?

Financial perspective is only one of the dimensions to be considered to ensure that a member's intellectual independence is not tarnished. After all, independent board members are expected to exercise inde-pendence with regard to their judgments and actions, to hold the cor-poration's interests at heart before all else, and be stakeholder-neutral in the course of making decisions. Consequently, the critical issue is intellectual and behavioral independence. The greater the board mem-bers exercise intellectual, political, or emotional independence in their judgments and behaviors, the higher their value to the board.

- One of the components of independence is **intellectual independ-ence**, the ability to make judgments without being dominated by others. For example, within a board whose members cannot be considered as peers owing to a distinct advantage of one or more members over others in terms of sector knowledge and/or management experience, it is likely that some members will refrain from expressing their opinions, which may seriously damage their independence.

- Another component of independence is **political independence**. The key to independence is to put the interests of the corporation above any of its stakeholders *per se*. If a political aspiration influences a member's judgments, this too will seriously damage their independence. For example, if a member who wishes to become, say, the local mayor puts his political aspirations above the interests of the corporation, they cannot be deemed to be independent. Similarly, if an individual has the potential to utilize their role on the board to get a more influential position with one of the stakeholders, this also would be an impediment to his/her independence.

- A third element of independence is **group independence**. If the candidate is a member of a family, sect, cast, or any other group where their decisions can be influenced by the leader of such a family, sect, cast, or group which may have a relationship with the company, then they cannot be deemed to be independent. Table 1.2 shows the prevalence of non-family, independent members of the boards of top family-run companies.

- Yet another component of independence is **emotional independence**. For example, if membership of that particular board is the basis of substantial social prestige for the individual, it may be difficult to exercise independent judgment in opposition to general thinking on the board.

In evaluating the independence of an individual, one has to take into consideration every dimension of independence – financial, intellectual, political, group, and emotional.

One danger in carrying the independence argument too far is eliminating qualified candidates who may serve the corporation well and going instead for people who have no relevant experience. Obviously, every individual, especially if they are successful, has numerous relationships. Therefore, having relationships with current or potential stakeholders of the company cannot and should not be a justification for removing a candidate from the eligibility list. What is important is

Table 1.2 Number of Independent Board Members Among International Family-Run Companies

Company	Rank among family-run businesses	Percentage of independent board members
Wal-Mart	1	64
Ford Motor	2	75
Samsung	3	54
LG Group	4	43
Carrefour	5	86
Fiat Group	6	53
Peugeot Citroen	8	25
BMW	12	15
Bosch	15	40
J. Sainsbury	22	75
Roche	28	69
Bombardier	36	69

how they behave if and when there is a potential area of conflict. The best guide for this is the track record of the individual. Evaluating the independence of each individual member is a delicate task that needs to be done on a regular basis, by their peers, based on the behavior and judgments of the individual and in the light of the understanding outlined above.

BEHAVIORS EXPECTED OF BOARD MEMBERS

A board must be provided with appropriate members, structure, and processes so as to ensure that its members can fulfill their main duties of guidance, decision-making, and oversight. Board members who are chosen according to the match between their character, their competencies, and the corporation's needs are expected to exercise independent judgment, and demonstrate certain behaviors in fulfilling their duties, as follows:

- **Knowing the corporation and the market well** Knowledge of the corporation's past and current positioning, strengths and weaknesses, threats and opportunities, culture and potential, is critically important for providing guidance and oversight. Further key requirements for board membership are a sound understanding of the current playing field and its dynamics, and not refraining from exercising judgment about the future.

- **Implementing a challenging and constructive questioning process** The main goal of this process should be to attain a good grasp of the corporation's circumstances and to ensure that every aspect of a decision is considered, rather than displaying one's knowledge, testing the management, or going through the motions of demonstrating compliance.

- **Having a good understanding of the corporation's cash flow** In order for a corporation to protect its assets and value, cash flow is just as important as its profit and loss statement. Inconsistencies that may arise between the cash situation and profit-and-loss situation must be well understood. For example, if an increase in sales is accomplished by increasing the payment terms, one should not be satisfied with the initial increase in profits, but also need also to evaluate the financial risks of increasing the working capital requirements as well as the risks of customer defaults.

- **Having an understanding of benchmarks** The corporation's performance should be evaluated in comparison with its competitors' performances, as well as with the budget, and with past years' performances. Performance evaluations should not be limited to financial indicators, but should also include measures such as process productivity; customer, supplier and employer satisfaction; and measures related to strategic initiatives. One of the keys to learning and continuous improvement is to seek comparisons with "best-in-class" examples.

- **Focusing not only on the performance of the current term, but also on the indicators for future performance** Areas that constitute risk for the future must be determined and managed. For this reason, conducting scenario analyses could help the mental preparation of members for encountering and dealing with risk factors. Such work may be conducted by management and the results shared with the board.

- **Inorganic growth opportunities** Board members have to be up-to-date in their information and understanding of the takeover targets and the risks associated with the market for corporations.

- **Succession planning** One of the key risks for a company is an unexpected change in key management positions. Therefore, the board should be concerned not only with the performance of the management, but also with succession planning. This process involves both identifying and following internal and external candidates as well as establishing development plans for internal candidates.

- **Potential off-balance-sheet liabilities** The board has to be aware of the contractual obligations, promises, and guarantees of the corporation. For this reason, distributor agreements, salary/bonus agreements made with senior management, and other agreements made with third parties need to be systematically evaluated by the board members.

- **Reputational risks** Companies are evaluated not only according to their financial results but also according to their adherence to legal requirements and ethical expectations. Therefore, having an adequate internal control system is important. The establishment of a continuous monitoring system, and systematic review by an internal audit department that has direct access to the board, are important. Also, having a dependable whistle blowing process is useful in identifying potential risks of fraud. Board members should have sufficient contact with management and employees at different levels to evaluate the risks.

- **Understanding customer expectations** Firsthand experience with the products and services of the company and interactions with customers are important inputs if sound judgments are to be made by board members.

- **Understanding the value chain** A sound understanding of each link in the value chain and its alternatives, and where the value added is captured throughout the entire commercial ecosystem (suppliers, sales channels and so on) is useful in making appropriate assessments of the corporation's risks. The strength of a chain is determined by the strength of its weakest link.

- **License to operate** Companies do not operate in vacuum. Their activities have direct and indirect effects on the communities they operate in. The responsibility of a corporation is broader than what the regulations ask for. Hence, sincerity and effectiveness in the exercise of corporate social responsibility are important in gaining the goodwill of the community. Board members should therefore provide effective oversight for corporate social responsibility (CSR) activities as well.

- **Being aware of potential regulatory and legislative changes** Companies are obliged to adhere to the legal and regulatory requirements in each jurisdiction. Therefore, having a proper understanding both of the current situation and of potential changes in it is an important input to exercising sound judgment and protecting the company against regulatory risks.

- **Understanding of the priorities and concerns of the investment community stakeholders** This, especially understanding the expectations of shareholders, is the top priority when it comes to meeting their expectations.

THE CHAIRPERSON

The chairperson runs the board, determines its priorities, and sets the agenda for meetings. Obviously, in doing so, he/she gets input from the CEO and other board members, particularly committee chairpersons. The CEO, in turn, manages the company and is accountable for corporate performance. The two most important duties of the chairperson are to ensure the effectiveness of the board and to ensure the sustainable increase of the corporation's value. The chairperson is responsible for timely and adequate communication between the board members and the management to ensure that there is a climate of trust and a preparedness to exercise sound judgments about key issues for the company.

An effective chairperson should be a role model of integrity, consistency, fairness, leadership, and adherence to governance principles. A key aspect of being a successful independent chairperson is not to have an ambition to replace the CEO. Such humility is key to a trustful relationship with the CEO.

Duties of the Chairperson of the Board

- To ensure timely and clear exchange of information between board members and management, so that the board may closely follow the corporation's performance, make suggestions that will increase the corporation's success rate and make sound judgments on key issues.

- To establish a positive and constructive climate of communication with the management, and ensure there is an open dialogue to adequately challenge the management proposals.

- To ensure that the board agenda contains items of relevance and value to directors, that the annual agenda covers all relevant dimensions, and that the board's time is managed properly,

- To ensure that board members are kept informed of the company's progress in implementing strategic decisions.

- To allocate sufficient time during board meetings to discuss each item fully.

- To ensure that issues are considered from different stakeholder perspectives and different angles prior to decision-making.

- To encourage directors to ask questions and express their views at board meetings.

- To ensure that the board comes to decisions once agenda items have been adequately discussed.

- To hold an in-camera executive session at the end of each board meeting to receive frank feedback from board members.

- To ensure an adequate orientation program for each new board member so that they may expeditiously become a fully functioning member.

- To ensure that the board in its entirety, all board members, and all committees are subjected to performance evaluations at least once a year.

- To identify skills gaps on the board and plan to overcome them, as well as to ensure that the board works as an effective team.

- To ensure that the activities of the committees established within the board are effective and that their respective mandates are clear.

In general, the chairperson of the board of directors and the CEO are two separate people. The relationship between the chairperson and the CEO is very important for the effective functioning of the board. The chairperson's role is not to manage, but to foster cooperation, to improve the flow of information, and to serve as a mentor to help the CEO manage the company.

The chairperson of the board needs to possess five main leadership characteristics, as follows:

- **Integrity and high standards of ethical conduct** They are trusted not to use information, or allow it to be used, in a misleading manner; openly recognize the contributions of others; are trusted to stand behind board decisions; and show no tolerance of unethical behavior.

- **Openness, transparency and accountability** The chairperson promotes effective sharing of information and expectations; has the respect of colleagues and management; and communicates effectively with different audiences.

- **Common sense and strategic thinking skills** They possess sufficient experience and skills to understand the competitive environment and risks; are able to cope well with uncertainty; and are able to lead the board to timely decision-making.

- **Team building** They are skillful in identifying, choosing, developing and motivating team members; have a track record of being able to work with those more skilled than themselves; are able to manage the differences within their team; are able to make the necessary investments to ensure the development of the people around them; and can lead by example.

- **Experience and knowledge** They are respected by the players in the value chain and stakeholders in the company, and understand their concerns.

"RIGHT PERSON" – SUMMARY

The quality of a board depends on the quality of its members, its structure, and its processes. This in turn is a function of the attitudes and behavior of the members as they conduct the business of the board. If the board of directors is trusted by all its stakeholders to conduct their business so as to ensure sustainable value creation by the company, then the board is composed of "the right people."

The board has to be a role model for applying the principles of corporate governance in its affairs so as to instill the right culture in the company, as follows:

Consistency A key element in gaining the trust of others is demonstrating consistency in behavior. This is true not only where the board is gaining the trust of stakeholders, but also where members of the board are gaining trust among themselves so as to create the proper climate to handle difficult decisions.

Responsibility As the board is the final decision-making authority for corporate decisions, the ability to take the initiative, to say "no," and to bring tough issues onto the agenda are valuable attributes for board members.

Accountability The board and its committees have to demonstrate humility, to conduct an annual self-evaluation process in order to identify areas for improvement in their own composition and operations, and to bring about the changes required.

Fairness The choice of a board member should not be based on their relationship with the chairperson, the CEO, or other members, but on the value they could add to the board. Also, in balancing the interest of various stakeholders, fairness is a key principle in gaining the trust of others.

Transparency Board members need to have the self-confidence and skill to be able to explain the basis of their decisions to each other and the management, in order to develop and maintain the right climate for raising challenging issues, and to help management internalize the reasoning of board decisions for better implementation.

Effectiveness Both the ability to demonstrate intellectual independence, so as to bring different perspectives to bear on board decisions, and regular benchmarking of both corporate and board performance, are essential for effectiveness.

Deployment Each member is expected to participate actively in board discussions, bring their experience to their judgments, and ensure effective communication with the management in order to ensure the deployment of the culture throughout the organization.

CHAPTER 2

Right Team

If everyone thinks the same, no one is thinking.

Walter Lipmann

DIVERSE PERSPECTIVES ON THE BOARD

A well-functioning board needs to balance two sets of competencies: a shared ability to provide guidance and oversight and an individual ability to bring different experiences and perspectives to the table to provide diversity and challenge. Each member of a functioning board needs to consider each other member as a peer with respect to their seniority and experience in order to work as an effective team, but at the same time members need to be able to bring different perspectives and be willing to challenge the management and other board members, so as to avoid groupthink. For example, a board whose members are all financially oriented may be less willing to challenge the management about other areas and prone to miss operational, political, or reputational risks.

Before identifying board member candidates it is better to identify which skills and competencies will be required by the company, and which skills gaps are present within the current board. This kind of approach is more likely to result in identifying the right pools of candidates and in making the right choices from among the candidates to form a balanced board with a comprehensive skills set and an appropriate diversity of experience. Table 2.1 shows how the various competencies of board members will relate to the board's responsibilities within the company.

Companies are dynamic structures. They are established, they grow, they mature, they are restructured, and sometimes they fail. The experience base needed to guide the corporation through these different phases may be different as well. The issues a start-up company needs to face may be very different from those met by a mature global company. Therefore, in order to maximize the fit, the composition of the board should be in harmony with the corporation's current status and future goals.

Table 2.1 Responsibilities of the Board and the Competencies of Board Members

Desired Qualities of Members of the Board	Ability to Think Strategically	Industry Experience	Top Management Experience	Senior-Level Relationships
Effective Utilization of Resources	••	•	••	
Guiding Strategy and Evaluating Business Results	•••	••	••	
Risk Management	••	•••	••	••
Guiding Senior Management and HR Development	•	•	•••	
Oversight of Audit and Internal Controls	••	•	••	•
Stakeholder Engagement (Partner, Investor, Society)	•	••	•	••

Competencies of Board Members vs. The Effects on the Responsibilities of the Board: • little, •• fair, ••• substantial.

FORMING SUCCESSFUL TEAMS

Life, like football, is a team sport.

Joe Namath

A collection of great players do not always make a great team, especially if they all excel at the same skills. There are numerous qualities that may be sought in board members and particular steps in the process of identifying the individuals who possess them. However, if the members' ability to work together and to complement each other's skills is not taken into explicit account, one may end up with a malfunctioning board. Building successful teams is an important entrepreneurial skill. Such a skill needs to be employed in forming the board as well. Any team needs the full commitment of each member to be successful. A board also needs the motivation, participation, and responsibility of each member to be successful.

Requirements for the Creation of a Successful Board

- A complete level of mutual respect, trust, and candor must be attained between all board members. Having a culture of transparency, openness, and the discipline for meeting preparation are key ingredients in creating an environment of trust.

- Even if each team member is a competent and senior individual, establishing an environment of trust requires spending time together and the exchange of ideas and views. The most important tool for developing communication and team spirit is ensuring access to relevant and meaningful information in a timely and synchronous fashion. If the management treats different board members differently in respect of the provision of information, this will damage the climate of trust.

- The board has to work as a unified team, not as individual stars. The differentiation of members based on their background, and especially the creation of a feeling of "insiders" (say, family members) and "the rest," is harmful to team spirit. The board should focus on value creation for the company and act as a team, not as individuals.

- Great care should be taken to ensure that the team is formed properly from the outset.

- Corporate incentive systems should be set up so as to increase team performance. From this perspective, board remuneration should also be team-based.

- Sufficient time has to be invested up front to ensure agreement on a common vision. Also, having a comprehensive orientation program for board members to make sure that they understand the environment and the competencies of the company is very helpful in reaching agreement on a common vision.

- Planned changes are necessary to ensure lasting team success. From time to time, responsibilities within the board need to be changed; and team performance can be enhanced through the introduction of new team members.

- The effectiveness of the board determines the effectiveness of the corporation. It is therefore worthwhile investing in building an effective board. Building an effective team requires agreement on a common vision, complementary skills, and thoughtful preparation.

AVOIDING COMMON PITFALLS

As the level of competition increases, so does the pressure to perform. This is true not for the management alone but for the directors as well. Adherence to corporate governance principles, or compliance with legislation, is not enough; the expectations of stakeholders go beyond that. Stakeholders expect innovation, strategic thinking, and the delivery of results. While achieving the status of a board member requires a significant amount of experience and respect, numerous boards that are made up of highly regarded individuals have been observed nevertheless to fall into the trap of common errors. Therefore, identifying some of these commonly made mistakes and the ways to avoid them should be instructive (see Table 2.2).

In short, the potential for common mistakes will diminish to the extent that the board members refrain from being emotional, base their judgments on facts in order to be objective, and encourage strategic flexibility.

Also, just like any decision-maker, a board needs to appreciate the fact that adopting too conservative an approach, in order to avoid mistakes at any cost, would result in indecisiveness and missed opportunities. What is important is learning from past mistakes and not repeating them.

AVOIDING GROUPTHINK

Insanity is an exception for individuals, but in groups it is the norm.

Nietzsche

Groupthink is a type of thought exhibited by group members who try to minimize conflict and reach consensus. Unless specific brainstorming techniques are utilized, people are influenced by others, especially if a number of them are of the same opinion, and their ability to consider alternatives may be hampered. In particular, groups with strong directive leadership, groups which are homogeneous and cohesive, and groups which are insulated from outside information and experts tend to exhibit groupthink without critically testing, analyzing, and evaluating ideas.

Another important subject is the way individuals process information. People obtain and use information in a myriad of ways. In processing information, people may feel obligated to behave differently in group discussions from how they do when they are alone.

Research conducted on the subject matter by Krishan Kumar,[1] regardless of whether individuals are family members or colleagues, states that, "they may rapidly take on one shape and cast their votes in one direction." And it is exactly for this reason that boards may be blind-sided.

In short, one of the risks a board faces is falling into the trap of groupthink. It should not be forgotten that if a board is made up

Table 2.2 Common Mistakes and How to Avoid Them

Mistake	How to Avoid It
Overconfidence of board members both in their own skills and in the capabilities of the company; assuming that their company is among the best run.	• Utilize scenario analyses to prepare for the worst. • Make risk evaluations and increasing sensitivity to the weak points identified in scenario analyses. • Make phased decisions to retain flexibility.
Delaying closure or disposal decisions for a nonperforming business because of the stigma of failure (applies especially to the boards of businesses within conglomerates).	• Reach a common understanding that putting an end to activities that drain value is the easiest way to create value. • Make realistic and independent assessments when considering disposal or closure, even if there were strong supporters and/or initiators of the business within the board.
Difficulty in overcoming the investment momentum once a major investment project starts may have heavy consequences for a corporation.	• Treat past expenditures as bygones and focus only on future expenditures. • Focus on value creation, in contrast to the difficulty of accepting the need to explain. • Phase investments, and make a plan which can be reviewed at certain predetermined points from the beginning in order to the minimize risk of a major failure.
Treating costs in different areas using different criteria.	• Treat the cost of a 1 million USD mistake made in marketing and the cost of a 1 million USD mistake in production using the same criteria. • Be especially careful when entering into a new and fashionable business, as being too eager and accepting a lower level of internal control standards may cost a great deal of money.
Being overly influenced by most recent developments. For example, a company that is caught by a recession with a high level of inventories may be too cautious for the upturn and lose market share when it is unable to meet rapidly increasing consumer demand.	• In a volatile environment, in making assumptions for the business plan, focus on long-term trends and averages, rather than the most recent experiences. • For learning purposes, conduct variance analyses to identify and measure the impact of various interactive developments. • Using comparative benchmarking data to get a more realistic understanding of the company's relative positioning would be useful for setting more realistic expectations. • In volatile environments increase flexibility and focus on the decision horizon, as this may be more appropriate than annual or multi-year plans. • Increasing the flexibility of the strategic plan, even if it costs more, may be more appropriate than making significant commitments that may be difficult to change.
Not tolerating different opinions and overemphasis on coherence, resulting in groupthink.	• Have a diverse board; a board that consists of members who have the same opinions on every subject need have no more than one member. • Establish a climate of candor and encourage dissent, which is useful for better risk and opportunity identification.

of members who all think alike then it means they possess only one independent member who creates any real value. Only board members who have different kinds of experience, and possess the self-confidence to express their opinions independently, ensure that different views are brought to bear.

Therefore, before members reach a joint decision, they should subject it to an assessment on their own.[2] On the other hand, a board's considering different perspectives and opinions should be no excuse for it not reaching a conclusion and a decision.

There are certain mistakes that increase the probability of a group falling into the trap of groupthink:

1. Not considering an adequate number of alternatives.

2. Not evaluating all of the dimensions of the alternatives.

3. Not being properly informed as to the risks and costs of each alternative.

4. Not giving enough attention to plans regarding implementation.

When the members of a group see themselves as being overly successful and invincible they are at an increased risk of falling into the trap of groupthink. This risk is seen more commonly in the boards of successful corporations who have been working together for long periods of time. When important decisions are being made it is not uncommon for some board members to take on the role of devil's advocate and also to weigh the opinions of experts other than members regarding the risks and alternatives; such actions may in fact decrease the risk of groupthinking.

One of the traps of groupthink is underestimating not only experts but also competitors. Boards that assume that experts do not assess subjects as well as they do may fall prey to selective listening and thus the inability to evaluate risk properly. The illusion of invulnerability may cause a board to underestimate the competition. Not being able to understand the basis of a competitor's moves not only obscures the weaknesses of one's position, but also may cause delays in taking remedies.

Another pitfall of groupthink is not taking into account facts that do not agree with one's own intellectual models. For this reason, paying attention to pieces of information that may contradict the prevailing assumptions, and seeking alternative explanations, may help reduce the risk of collective rationalization.

Board members may be more apt to exhibit similar thought patterns and more liable to making joint mistakes if they fall into the illusion of morality. Assuming that their values are the only correct ones, and neglecting different value judgments and perspectives, may cause groupthink. Therefore, if the board considers the effects of each decision on different stakeholders before reaching a conclusion on a decision, the risk of this illusion will decline.

One of the most important traps of groupthink is where an individual refrains from voicing differing opinions so as to be embraced by the group. This type of self-censorship is more frequently observed in groups that are steered by strong leaders who are apt to make quick decisions. For this reason, it is especially important that the chairperson of a board does not voice their own opinions prior to encouraging other members to express their views.

Boards may also fall into the trap of groupthink if members put pressure on dissenters to vote with the majority opinion. Dissent is not disloyalty and should not be treated as such. Therefore, one of the key responsibilities of the chairperson is to solicit and receive feedback from all members, so as to encourage the voicing of different perspectives, and to prevent such social pressure to be exerted on dissenters.

One of the deadly sins of management is to provide selective information to the board to lead them to a predetermined decision. Therefore, having a good understanding of the company's environment, asking for comparative data on competitors, and having access to independent information sources about general trends will help reduce such a risk. Bias in the selection of information provided is a terrible mistake, and contaminates the climate of trust in the boardroom.

None of us is as intelligent as all of us. For this reason, strategic decisions that involve important risks related to the future of a company need to be taken and/or confirmed by the board rather than by any one individual. This in turn needs a climate of candor, openness, and avoidance of groupthink to ensure that different aspects of the decision are tabled and the quality of the decisions increased.

THE NUMBER OF BOARD MEMBERS

The number of board members influences the effectiveness of decision-making. However, the right number of board members is a function of the circumstances and complexities of the corporation and its situation. The factors to be considered when assessing the corporation's needs include, but are not limited to:

- The geographic scope and complexity of the business.

- Committees to be established (and the need for independent committee members).

- The cost of the board to the corporation.

While boards vary in size, as the number of directors increases they encounter more coordination problems, and have difficulty developing effective communication and teamwork. When determining the ideal size of a board, the number of committees is one of the criteria.

As we can see in Table 2.3, a board may have from 7 to 15 members, depending upon the following: the number of committees; the maximum number of committees each member would serve in (assumed to be two); and the size of the committee (in the table assumed to be 3 or 5.)

The average size of the board of directors for the largest 20 global companies is 15 (see Figure 2.1). This is due to the complexity and geographic scope of these companies. Those companies that operate on a smaller scale with limited geographic scope are expected to have 7 to 11 board members. It is recommended that the majority of the board members be independent.

As the number of members of a board increases, it becomes more difficult for the board to establish coordination and take any necessary initiatives. Hence both the importance of director orientation programs and the dependence on committee work increase.

Table 2.3 Calculating the Number of Board Members

	Minimum	Maximum
Chairman	1	1
Executive/Dependent Member		2
Independent Member	6	12
Committee 1	3	5
Committee 2	3	5
Committee 3	3	5
Committee 4		5
Committee 5		5

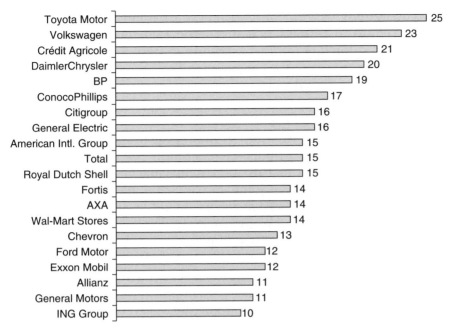

Figure 2.1 Fortune 500 (2006) Number of Board Members of the Top 20 Companies

"RIGHT TEAM" – SUMMARY

Board performance is a team performance and is key to corporate success. Aside from being the "right person" to provide guidance and oversight, each member has to act effectively as a team member so as to ensure that a good governance culture is established throughout the corporation. As a team, the board of directors has to have complementary skills and experience relevant to the corporation and be aware of the common pitfalls in joint decision-making, and take the necessary precautions to avoid groupthink.

Consistency An effective orientation program, spending time together with other members for team-building, and having a shared vision for the corporation are all key to have consistency in board decisions.

Responsibility Each member should be aware of their own individual responsibility to consider the quality of the information presented, the logic of the proposal, the potential consequences of the recommendations, and the judgment to be applied to reach a decision. The members should also be aware of their joint responsibility for creating an appropriate climate in the boardroom in order to avoid common decision-making pitfalls and groupthink.

Accountability As the board members are jointly accountable for their decisions, it follows that it is important to pay attention to avoiding the illusions of invulnerability, stereotyping, collective rationalization, pressure for cohesion, and self-censorship – not only in the thinking and conduct of each member, but also in the collective culture of the board.

Fairness Team members should not be treated differently with respect to access to information or management. At the same time, each member should feel obliged to share any relevant information obtained from sources other than the management with their fellow members so as to improve joint decision-making. The rewarding and/or remuneration of board members should be team-based.

Transparency Successful teams are created through the support of a management culture that encourages teamwork and transparent communications.

Effectiveness The diversity and complementarities of the experience and skills set of each member is an important tool for improving the effectiveness of board decision-making. Therefore, composition of the board should take these characteristics into account.

Deployment The concept of team-building is relevant not only for the board, but also for the management. Groups are better than individuals at making complex decisions, because they can provide new ideas, bring a variety of differing perspectives to bear, and act as error-correcting mechanisms. Therefore, the deployment of governance principles throughout the organization improves organizational decision-making processes.

NOTES

1   Jeff Weintraub and Krishan Kumar (eds.), *Public and Private in Thought and Practice: Perspectives on a Dichotomy*, University of Chicago Press, 1997.
2   Abigail W. Leonard, Study: Group Thinking Clouds Decision, Special to LiveScience, posted: 21 February 2007, www.livesciences.com/health/070221_friends_memory.html

CHAPTER 3

Right Processes

To open a shop is easy. Keeping it open is an art.

Chinese proverb

The success of a corporation depends on the effectiveness of its resource allocation decisions. Each decision has four components:

- Right to initiate.
- Right to approve.
- Right to implement.
- Right to monitor.

While right to initiate and right to implement are **management rights**, right to approve and right to monitor are **control rights**. Control rights also include the right to make an evaluation of the performance of management in exercising management rights. The segregation of management rights and control rights is the key to having an effective control system at each level of management.

In particular, for key top-level strategic decisions the control rights are exercised by the board of directors. Also, the right to initiate certain decisions – such as hiring, evaluating, compensating, and firing top executives and external auditors – should belong to the board of directors. The board has to get the approval of the shareholders in the annual shareholders' meeting, at least for their own compensation policies, in order to avoid any potential for conflict of interest, in utilizing their initiation rights for their own benefit.

To ensure that the board can fulfill this role properly, the board has to take control of its own processes and composition. One of the tools for the effective utilization of board members' time is to utilize board committees to address specific issues.

BOARD AGENDAS AND MEETINGS

The main goal of board meetings is twofold: to provide guidance and to provide oversight. Therefore, the board's agenda has to cover all the relevant issues for the company. Board meetings have to be effective in informing the board members about the issues the company is facing or is likely to face and in monitoring implementation of the previous decisions. The board's time has to be effectively utilized to provide the necessary and sufficient information, to allow sufficient discussion of every relevant aspect for decision-making, and to get to a closure on key decisions.

If directors are to function as a peer group and to provide guidance, they need to be kept fully informed about every major development. They should never feel that they are in the dark or be surprised. Getting the right information to board members at the right time is critical for any board's effectiveness.

First, ensuring attendance is of the utmost importance. Attendance can be increased through long-term planning. The dates, hours and locations of meetings can be set for the entire year, thereby allowing members ample time to plan their attendance in advance.

Aside from regular board meetings, board members should also meet in less formal settings, and spend time together at dinners or off-site retreats. Special retreats where strategy or business continuity plans are discussed, are particularly valuable. At some of these meetings, especially those where executive performance evaluations and annual reward decisions are made, in-camera sessions without management are useful.

Items on board meeting agendas may be classified under the following four headings:

1. Informing board members.

2. Considering proposals and providing guidance.

3. Decision-making.

4. Assigning responsibilities and monitoring results.

(See Table 3.1.)

Timely circulation of board presentations ahead of meetings helps the board members come to the meetings prepared. Similarly, circulating minutes soon after the meeting improves communication both among the board members, and with the management, and creates a culture of open communication.

It is highly recommended that the schedule of board meetings be set well in advance in order to be able to accommodate senior, experienced members, who are generally busy and prefer to plan ahead. Also, establishing the annual work agenda helps ensure that the main

Table 3.1 Meeting Agenda

Information	Guidance	Decision-Making	Oversight
Financial a. Credits–Receivables (size and maturity) b. Working capital c. Balance sheet/income statement/cash flow d. Budget comparison e. Developments in the economy and the financial markets f. Benchmarking g. M&A developments h. Other	To benefit from the views and experience of board members, opening the strategic plan and action plans to discussion is very useful. Guidance on potential risks and remedies increases the probability of success.	For issues that are brought to decision, priority has to be given to explaining the environment, the pros and cons of alternatives for each stakeholder, plus a cost–benefit analysis for the recommended approach as well as the action plan to be followed to control the risks. Sufficient time has then to be allocated to discussion before calling for a decision.	Oversight requires making clear assignments of responsibility for each action, as well as reviewing performance and internal–external audit findings.
Projects a. Plan vs. realization (cost, time, effectiveness) b. Investments/Joint ventures c. Obstacles–bottlenecks d. Potential projects e. Competitors' investments			
Internal developments a. Access to resources b. HR issues c. Efficiency improvements d. Benchmarks c. Internal controls			
Communication a. Investors b. Internal stakeholders c. External stakeholder c. Reports on committee work			
			Monitoring decisions made in previous meetings

issues for the organization are properly addressed by the board. Having 5 to 7 regular board meetings annually is common practice. It is also good practice to set aside a separate meeting at which to review corporate strategy and risk management, and to make sure that at least once a year the performance of the board committees and the board as a whole is evaluated.

Board meetings should be planned to address the following:

- Issues deemed to be important by the CEO and top management.
- Issues that committee chairpersons may wish to bring to the attention of the full board.
- The corporation's strategic priorities.
- Risk mitigation actions for the important risk areas for the corporation.
- Internal control systems.
- The approval and monitoring of the budget.
- Major investment decisions.
- Mergers and acquisitions.
- The corporation's stock performance.
- Performance evaluations and the compensation of senior executives.
- New business, market, and product development opportunities.

The chairperson is responsible for setting the agenda for board meetings, taking into account the recommendations of the CEO, committee chairpersons, and any other board member. The agenda should focus on key strategic issues, rather than day-to-day operational issues, which are the responsibility of the management. Board meetings are run by the chairperson of the board. It is the responsibility of the chairperson to prioritize items to be put on the agenda and to allocate adequate time for discussion and consideration, so that the board members feel comfortable reaching a conclusion.

The agenda and meeting materials have to be provided to the board members prior to the meeting to enable adequate preparation. Additional plant visits, market visits, and contacts with customers and other stakeholders are useful for board members and help board members to exercise judgment on corporate priorities and performance.

Other special meetings may be called if certain issues require the board to be involved, such as an M&A transaction. To the extent possible, such meetings should be announced sufficiently in advance so that non-executive members can get prepared.

The board's activities, a general description of its performance, and the attendance record of its members are expected to be reported annually, especially in the case of public companies.

The following is an example of notes on agenda from General Electric:

Agenda Setting

The board shall be responsible for its agenda. At the December board meeting, the CEO and the presiding director will propose for the board's approval key issues of strategy, risk and integrity to be scheduled and discussed during the course of the next calendar year. Before that meeting, the board will be invited to offer its suggestions. As a result of this process, a schedule of major discussion items for the following year will be established. Prior to each board meeting, the CEO will discuss the other specific agenda items for the meeting with the presiding director, who shall have authority to approve the agenda for the meeting. The CEO and the presiding director, or committee chair as appropriate, shall determine the nature and extent of information that shall be provided regularly to the directors before each scheduled board or committee meeting. Directors are urged to make suggestions for agenda items, or additional pre-meeting materials, to the CEO, the presiding director, or appropriate committee chair at any time.

MINUTES

The **minutes** are an important tool for internal communication and they serve as a legal record of the due process exhibited by the board in making judgment calls on behalf of the shareholders. Minutes are also a good tool for monitoring the implementation of previous decisions.

Effective use of the minutes may in fact increase the effectiveness of the board as well. The minutes of board meetings establish a record of the alternatives considered and the rationale of the decisions taken. They establish the critical thinking process exhibited by the board for each decision and so demonstrate that the board handles its duty to care effectively.

Records of board decisions could also serve as a valuable input in evaluating the effectiveness of the board in determining priorities, time management, and annual self-evaluations of board performance.

There is no single standard for keeping minutes of board meetings. While some organizations prefer to keep detailed records of all the discussions, others prefer to summarize the board's decisions. Both practices have their pros and cons. Minutes that document only the board's decisions are shorter and easier to record, but they do not say much about the information or the rationale that the decisions were based on. On the other hand, minutes covering every conversation that took place during a board meeting are not only tedious but may also be subject to different interpretations if and when they become part of legal proceedings. Tape recordings of the meetings have drawbacks similar to those of the full minutes. Therefore, minutes that strike a balance between the short form and the full are often the most effective.

What the Minutes Should Record

1. Who attended the meeting and how (by telephone or in person).

2. When and at what time the meeting took place, and what basic agenda topics were discussed (it may be beneficial to note how much time was set aside for each item).

3. The type of meeting and how the meeting was announced. (A regular meeting that was previously agreed upon, or an extraordinary meeting? A meeting consisting of all board members, or a committee meeting?)

4. Whether there was an executive session where management was not present.

5. What information was shared with attendees, when such information was presented, and the opinions of members as to whether they found the information sufficient.

6. Which alternatives and dimensions were considered by the board, and whether there were any dissenting views.

7. Indicators of independent assessments made by members, and decisions taken with due consideration.

8. Decisions made and the rationale behind them.

9. The dissenting opinions of members who did not agree with decisions (if any).

10. Whether there were any members who exempted themselves from a decision because of a potential conflict of interest.

It is good practice to establish a document retention policy, in order to ensure that material presented to the board remains confidential. As the notes taken by each member may not be complete, and may reflect only their own perspective, it is important to have the minutes taken by the corporate secretary, to be approved by the next meeting of the board. It is also good practice, at the next board meeting, to review the previous meeting's decisions and to have a management discussion about the developments arising from them.

BOARD COMMITTEES

Committees are formed to enable board members to use their expertise to address key board issues such as audit, nomination, performance evaluation, and compensation in more depth than regular board meetings normally allow. Committees do not replace the role of the board but present their findings and recommendations to the full board for decision. While the number and the complexity of the issues covered by the committees vary by company, industry, or jurisdiction, committees are commonly constituted for:

- Audit.
- Governance.
- Compensation.
- Safety.
- Social responsibility.

In Table 3.2, the top 20 global companies found in the Fortune 500 (2006) and their committees are listed.

- The number of committees varies between 2 and 7; the average being 4.
- Among the top 20 companies' boards:
  - 100% have audit committees.
  - 55% have a nominating and governance committee.
  - 80% have a compensation committee.
  - 45% have a social responsibility and public policy committee.

Table 3.2 Committees Present in the Top 20 Corporations in the Fortune 500 List (2006)

	Audit	Risk & Capital	Compensation[a]	Nominating & Governance[b]	Social Responsibility[c]	Finance	Executive	Strategic Planning & Finance[d]	Board Affairs[e]	Chairman[f]	Mediation	Other
Exxon Mobil	•		•		•	•	•		•			Advisory Committee on Contributions
Wal-Mart Stores	•		•				•	•				Stock Options
Royal Dutch Shell	•		•	•	•							
BP	•		•	•						•		Ethics and Environment Assurance
General Motors	•		•	•	•							Investment Funds
Chevron	•		•	•	•							
DaimlerChrysler	•									•	•	
Toyota Motor	na											
Ford Motor	•		•	•	•	•						

	a	b	c	d	e	f	Standing	Regulatory, Compliance and Legal
ConocoPhillips	•	•	•					
General Electric	•	•	•	•				
Total	•		•					
ING Group	•		•					
Citigroup	•		•	•	•			
AXA	•	•	•	•		•		
Allianz	•			•			•	
Volkswagen	•	•					•	
Fortis	•		•					
Crédit Agricole	•	•	•			•		
AIG	•		•	•	•			

[a] Remuneration. [b] Nomination & Succession, Personnel, Appoints. [c] Public Issues, Public Policy. [d] Strategic. [e] Directors Affairs. [f] Chairman's.

Apart from these, in order to meet the needs of the company or to fulfill the legal requirements of the relevant jurisdiction, additional committees are formed. For example: German-based companies have a "mediation committee," Wal-Mart has a "stock option committee," and General Motors has an "investment funds committee."

The fundamental objectives of the most frequently observed committees are as follows:

- **Audit** To review financial statements and internal controls and recommend the appointment of external auditors. Integrity of disclosures and fraud prevention are also addressed by this committee.

  ○ To provide leadership for internal audit and internal control departments.

  ○ To recommend independent external auditors and approve their compensation.

  ○ To evaluate performance of independent external auditors on the basis of objectivity, independence, and effectiveness.

  ○ To ensure open communication between internal and external auditors and the board.

  ○ To report their findings and their work and make recommendation, to improve disclosure standards and internal control systems to the full board. (See Chapter 7 for more about audit committees.)

- **Nominating and governance** To ensure that the board, CEO, and key members of the management have the necessary skills, experience and are motivated, and that there is an explicit process to identify, recruit, and develop people for these positions. The nomination and governance committee's work focuses on three levels:

  ○ *The Board*

    ○ To ensure that there is a properly constituted board whose members together have the necessary experience and skills to provide stewardship to the business.

    ○ To ensure that the appropriate structure, composition, mandate, and membership are established and reviewed annually for each board committee.

    ○ To ensure that the members' experience is properly utilized in committee assignments.

- To ensure that there is a continuity plan which includes identification of necessary skills for issues the company is likely to face and a pipeline of potential candidates with such skills, as well as a track record of integrity, diversity, knowledge, and judgment.

- To ensure that there is a satisfactory orientation program for new members.

- To conduct a regular assessment of the board's effectiveness and a match of the board's skills set with the requirements of the business.

- To ensure that an evaluation of the chairperson's and individual members' performance is done on an annual basis, and feedback provided to each.

- To assess the adequacy of the board and committee meetings for the purposes of the company.

- To monitor best practices for governance to conform to the highest standards of governance.

- To report on performance and developments regarding the board to the shareholders.

- *Top management*

    - To ensure that that the corporation has capable, motivated top management.

    - To ensure that top management has what is needed to deliver stretch targets.

    - To ensure that there is a succession planning system.

    - To ensure that there is sufficient depth in the management team and that there is a development plan for high potentials with sufficient resources.

    - To ensure that there is an objective performance evaluation system.

- *Human resources policies for all employees*

    - To ensure that the corporation has appropriate human resources management policies (such as recruitment, performance management, career development, compensation, and reward systems) and that they are applied consistently and benchmarked on a regular basis for the purpose of identifying and implementing improvements.

- ○ To ensure that the corporation has a right-sized workforce, with the appropriate knowledge, experience, skills sets, performance, and motivation.

- ○ To ensure that key positions are identified and that the skills, performance criteria, development plans, and continuity plans are present and applied.

- ○ To ensure that the human resources effectiveness indicators for the entire organization are identified and the performance is tracked.

- **Compensation**   Helps the full board in fulfilling one of its main responsibilities, namely of overseeing corporate performance and assuring itself of the quality, integrity, depth, and continuity of management, ensuring the motivation and loyalty of management with a competitive compensation system.

  - ○ To determine the structure and policies for the company's executive compensation system and to review them annually for competitiveness.

  - ○ To determine the structure and policies of the board compensation system and to review them for competitiveness.

  - ○ To determine annual and long-term goals for performance-based remuneration systems.

  - ○ To conduct performance appraisals for top management and make recommendations to the board with respect to rewarding the top management.

  - ○ To review the contracts of advisors to the board on an annual basis.

  - ○ To review the charter of the committee annually.

- **Safety and social responsibility**   To review the safety, health, environmental, and community affairs programs and performance of the company; to provide oversight to ensure that the activities of the corporation are conducted in accordance with the stated policies, and to assess the results of such activities.

In order to assure that each committee runs smoothly it is necessary for each committee to have its own "committee charter," an example of which is the following:

Charter of the Compensation Committee, Ford Motor Co.

Charter of the Compensation Committee of the Board of Directors

I. Purpose

The Compensation Committee shall:

- Assist the Board of Directors in discharging its responsibility to the shareholders with respect to the Company's compensation programs, compensation of the Company's executives and identify qualified individuals to become Company officers; and

- Review the annual Compensation Discussion and Analysis to be included in the Company's annual proxy statement, and produce an annual report of the Compensation Committee on executive compensation for inclusion in the Company's annual proxy statement, in accordance with applicable rules and regulations.

II. Structure and Operations

Composition and Qualifications The Compensation Committee shall be comprised of two or more directors as determined by the Board (upon the recommendation of the Nominating and Governance Committee), each of whom is determined by the Board to be an "independent" director in accordance with the rules of the New York Stock Exchange and any other applicable legal or regulatory requirement. Additionally, no director may serve on the Compensation Committee unless he or she satisfies the requirements of an "outside director" for purposes of Section 162(m) of the Internal Revenue Code.

Appointment and Removal The members of the Compensation Committee shall be designated by the Board annually and shall serve until such member's successor is duly designated or until such member's earlier resignation or removal. Any member of the Compensation Committee may be removed from the Committee, with or without cause, by a majority vote of the Board. Unless a Chair is designated by the Board, the members of the Compensation Committee shall designate a Chair by majority vote of the full Compensation Committee membership. The Chair will chair all regular sessions of the Compensation Committee and set the agendas for Compensation Committee meetings.

Delegation to Subcommittees In fulfilling its responsibilities, the Compensation Committee shall be entitled to delegate any or all of its responsibilities to a subcommittee of the Compensation Committee and, to the extent not expressly reserved to the Compensation Committee by the Board or by applicable law, rule or regulation, to any other committee of directors of the Company appointed by it, which may or may not be composed of members of the Compensation Committee.

III. Meetings

The Compensation Committee shall ordinarily meet at least four times annually, or more frequently as circumstances dictate. Any member of the Compensation Committee may call meetings of the Compensation Committee.

As part of its review and establishment of the performance criteria and compensation of designated key executives, the Compensation Committee should meet separately at least on an annual basis with the Chief Executive Officer, the Company's Group Vice President – Corporate Human Resources and Labor Affairs, and any other Company officers it deems appropriate. However, the Compensation Committee may meet without such officers present, and in all cases such officers shall not be present at meetings at which their performance or compensation is being discussed or determined.

Any director of the Company who is not a member of the Compensation Committee may attend meetings of the Compensation Committee; provided, however, that any director who is not a member of the Compensation Committee may not vote on any matter coming before the Compensation Committee for a vote. The Compensation Committee also may invite to its meetings any member of management of the Company and such other persons as it deems appropriate in order to carry out its responsibilities. The Compensation Committee may meet in executive session, as the Compensation Committee deems necessary or appropriate.

IV. Responsibilities and Duties

The following functions shall be common recurring activities of the Compensation Committee in carrying out its purpose set forth in Section I of this Charter. These functions should serve as a guide with the understanding that the Compensation Committee may carry out additional functions and adopt additional policies and procedures as may be appropriate in light of changing business, legislative, regulatory, legal or other conditions. The Compensation Committee shall also carry out any other responsibilities and duties delegated to it by the Board from time to time related to the purpose of the Compensation Committee set forth in Section I of this Charter.

The Compensation Committee, in discharging its oversight role, is empowered to study or investigate any matter of interest or concern within the purpose of the Compensation Committee that the Compensation Committee deems appropriate or necessary and shall have the sole authority to retain and terminate outside counsel or other experts for this purpose, including the authority to approve the fees payable to such counsel or experts and any other terms of retention.

To fulfill its responsibilities and duties, the Compensation Committee shall:

Compensation for Executive Officers/Officer Selection/Conflicts

- Establish and review the overall executive compensation philosophy of the Company.

- Review and approve Company goals and objectives relevant to CEO and other executive officers' compensation, including annual performance objectives.

- Evaluate the performance of the CEO and other executive officers in light of established goals and objectives and, based on such evaluation, review and approve the annual salary, bonus, stock options, other incentive awards and other benefits, direct and indirect, of the CEO and other executive officers.

- Identify individuals qualified to become officers, and recommend the selection of candidates for all officer positions to be filled by the Board.

- In connection with executive compensation plans:

  ○ Review and recommend to the full Board, or approve as appropriate, new executive compensation plans and any changes to or modifications of existing executive compensation plans;

  ○ Review on a periodic basis the operations of the Company's executive compensation programs to determine whether they are properly coordinated and achieving their intended purposes;

  ○ Establish and periodically review policies for the administration of executive compensation programs; and

  ○ Take steps to modify any executive compensation program that, upon analysis, is determined to yield compensation or benefits that are not reasonably related to executive and corporate performance.

  ○ Establish and periodically review policies in the area of senior management perquisites.

  ○ Review and make recommendations to the Board, or approve, as appropriate, any contracts or other transactions with current or former executive officers of the Company and any nonindependent director, including consulting arrangements, employment contracts, and severance or termination arrangements.

○ Consider questions of independence and requests of current and former officers to engage in activities with other companies.

Monitoring Incentive, Equity-Based and other Compensation Plans and Programs

- Perform duties delegated to it by the Board under various executive compensation plans.

- Review and make recommendations to the full Board, or approve, as appropriate, all awards of stock, stock options and other incentive compensation awards and other compensation to executive officers pursuant to the Company's executive plans and programs.

- Monitor compliance by executives with the terms and conditions of the Company's executive compensation plans.

- Select, retain, terminate and/or replace, as needed, compensation and benefits consultants and other outside experts to provide independent advice to the Compensation Committee. In that connection, in the event the Compensation Committee retains a compensation consultant or other expert, or if the Company should retain a compensation consultant or other expert to assist in the evaluation of CEO or senior executive compensation, the Compensation Committee shall have the sole authority to approve such consultant's or expert's fees and other retention terms.

Reports

- Review the annual Compensation Discussion and Analysis for inclusion in the Company's proxy statement, and prepare an annual report on executive compensation for inclusion in the Company's proxy statement, in accordance with applicable rules and regulations.

- Report regularly to the Board (i) following meetings of the Compensation Committee, (ii) with respect to such other matters as are relevant to the Compensation Committee's discharge of its responsibilities and (iii) with respect to such recommendations as the Compensation Committee may deem appropriate. The report to the Board may take the form of an oral report by the Chair or any other member of the Compensation Committee designated by the Compensation Committee to make such report.

- Maintain minutes and other records of meetings and activities of the Compensation Committee, as appropriate under Delaware law.

At a minimum the charter should be comprised of:

- Mission.
- Membership and structure.
- Activities.
- Assessment.
- Reporting.

Committees usually have members that range in number between 3 to 9 (see Table 3.3). In general, in order for members to strike a balance

Table 3.3 Number of Committee Members

	Audit	Management Compensation	Management Development & Governance	Social Responsibility	Finance	Other
Royal Dutch Shell	3	3	3	3		
BP	6	5	4			4[a]
General Motors	4	4	5	2		5[b]
Chevron	4	4	5	5		
Ford Motor	4	3	8	5	6	
General Electric	5	5	7	9		
Total	3	3				
AXA	5	5	4		4	
AIG	3	4	4	3	4	4[c]

[a]Ethics & Environment Trust; [b]Investment Funds Committee; [c]Regulatory Committee.

between workload and responsibilities, members serve on no more than two committees.

The membership criteria for each committee differ. For example, while it is expected that the chairperson and members of the audit committee will be independent and have a high degree of financial literacy, and that at least one member will have accounting expertise, the members of the compensation committee should be independent non-executives.

THE SELECTION OF BOARD MEMBERS

The process of selecting board members is initiated with the corporate governance committee by determining the prospective candidates and presenting them to the board for approval. The board, at each annual shareholders' meeting, presents the shareholders with a list of potential candidates for the next term and the shareholders elect the members of the board during the general assembly meeting. If and when a vacancy occurs at the board, these positions may be filled by the board until the next general assembly takes place.

The corporate governance committee identifies the main issues to be faced by the corporation, the skills gap within the current board, and the key competencies expected from the candidates; gets the approval of the full board on these matters, and then, either through a consultant or directly, draws up a list of candidates potentially fulfilling these requirements; prioritizes the candidates according to their fit to the predetermined criteria, checks the references, and approaches them to assess the appropriateness of their skills and experience, as well as their willingness to join the board. Then according to this evaluation the committee makes a formal proposal to the full board for the new member.

Once this is approved the chairperson and/or lead director along with one independent member approaches the candidate and makes an offer to join the board. In this meeting the following items have to be covered:

- The role and responsibilities of a board member.
- Any potential conflicts of interest and impediments to independence.
- The time required for being an effective board member for this company.
- The compensation system for the board members.
- Term of service.
- Main issues of the corporation and the role expected from the candidate.
- The orientation program and the board schedule.

A typical BP board attendance report can be seen on pp. 46–7.

BOARD PERFORMANCE EVALUATIONS

In order to identify areas for improvement and take actions to improve board performance, the board should allocate sufficient time to reviewing their own performance, including the performance of board committees, on an annual basis. The results should be circulated to the members, either by the chairperson or by the lead director.

The following subjects should be considered during the evaluations:

- **For the board as a whole**

  - Reaching goals.

  - Contributions made to development, and scrutiny of corporate strategies.

  - Contributions made to the risk management architecture.

  - Approach to problems and crises.

  - Appropriateness of the agenda.

  - Evaluation of the alignment of top executives and human resources with the strategies.

  - Communication within the board.

  - Communication with the management and stakeholders.

- **For the chairperson of the board**

  - Effective leadership of the board.

  - Shareholder relations.

  - Relations and communication within the board.

  - The effectiveness of the process to ensure that the board agenda addresses the right issues.

- **For board members**

  - Meeting preparation and attendance record.

  - The quality of contributions made to corporate strategy and risk management.

The board requires all members to devote sufficient time to the work of the attend meetings.

In addition to the AGM (which 14 directors attended), the board met nine Two of these meetings were two-day strategy discussions. A number of their attendance by board members are shown in the table below.

	Board Meetings		Audit Committee Meetings		SEEAC Meetings	
	Attended	Possible	Attended	Possible	Attended	Possible
P D Sutherland	9	9	–	–	–	–
J H Bryan	9	9	10	12	–	–
A Burgmans	9	9	–	–	6	7
Sir William Castell	3	3	1	2	2	2
E B Davis, Jr	7	9	11	12	–	–
D J Flint	9	9	11	12	–	–
Dr. D S Julius	8	9	–	–	–	–
Sir Tom Mckillop	9	9	–	–	4	4
Dr. W E Massey	9	9	–	–	7	7
H M P Miles	4	4	3	4	1	3
Sir Ian Prosse	9	9	11	12	–	–
M H Wilson	2	2	3	3	2	2
Lord Browne	9	9	–	–	–	–
Dr. A B Hayward	9	9	–	–	–	–
Dr. D C Allen	9	9	–	–	–	–
I C Conn	9	9	–	–	–	–
Dr. B E Grote	9	9	–	–	–	–
J A Manzoni	9	9	–	–	–	–

- Relations with board members and senior management.
- Communication skills in presenting opinions/views.
- Contributions to activities outside of board meetings.
- Creating trust and respect with performance and behavior.

Report (*BP Annual Report*, 2006)

board to discharge the office of director and to use their best endeavors to

times during 2006: six times in the UK, twice in the US and once in Turkey.
board committee meetings were held during the year. Details of these and

Chairman's Committee Meetings		Renumeration Committee Meetings		Nomination Committee Meetings	
Attended	Possible	Attended	Possible	Attended	Possible
4	4	5	5	6	6
4	4	5	5	–	–
4	4	–	–	–	–
1	1	–	–	–	–
3	4	4	5	–	–
4	4	–	–	–	–
3	4	5	5	6	6
4	4	5	5	–	–
4	4	–	–	6	6
0	1	–	–	–	–
4	4	5	5	6	6
1	1	–	–	–	–
–	–	–	–	–	–
–	–	–	–	–	–
–	–	–	–	–	–
–	–	–	–	–	–
–	–	–	–	–	–
–	–	–	–	–	–

- Possession of knowledge about the industry and market conditions.

- Understanding of corporate governance and financial reporting requirements.

- **For the board processes**
  - Effectiveness of presentation of information to the board.
  - Effectiveness of agenda-setting.
  - Timeliness of decision-making.
  - Adequacy of board and committee meetings. In particular the following areas have to be evaluated with respect to the attention they get from the board:
    - Adoption of a strategic planning process.
    - A process for identifying major risk areas (in strategic, operational, leadership, partnerships, and reputation dimensions), and ensuring that adequate mitigation strategies and systems are implemented.
    - Succession planning, including development plans for senior management and monitoring progress as well as compensation policies, to ensure the ability to attract and retain a high-quality management team.
    - Communication and disclosure policies with authorities, investors, analysts, and press.
    - Integrity of internal control and management information systems, including assurance of the independence of the outside auditors and the availability of a fair and independent whistle-blowing process.
    - Adoption of a self-evaluation process for the board covering the areas of composition, processes, up-to-date and relevant information availability, culture and climate, and learning for continuous improvement. Table 3.4 presents a sample board self-evaluation form.

BOARD COMPENSATION PACKAGES

The responsibility for establishing the board compensation system is generally given to the compensation committee, and if there is not a compensation committee, then the responsibility falls within the governance committee mandate. The committee presents its preparations

Table 3.4 Sample Board Performance Evaluation Form[3]

The evaluation form covers the following key areas:

- Do we have the right people?
- Do they function as an effective team?
- Do we have the right processes?
- Do we get timely and relevant information?
- Do we have the right culture?
- Are we providing the right kind of guidance?
- Are we providing adequate oversight?
- Are we reviewing our business results and other benchmarks to continually improve our performance?

Along with the answers to these questions, members are expected to provide examples and suggestions for improvement on subjects that they find successful and/or unsuccessful.

I. Do we have the right people?	Strongly Disagree	Disagree	Neutral	Agree	Strongly Agree
1. All the board members possess the basic requirements to effectively add value. (For example: Demonstrate integrity and high ethical standards. Have career experience and expertise relevant to the corporation's business purpose, financial responsibilities and risk profile. Have a proven track record and understanding of fiduciary duty. Have financial literacy. Demonstrate well-developed listening, communicating and influencing skills so that the individual directors can actively participate in board discussions and debate. Devote sufficient time and attention to assume the responsibilities to serve as a director.)	1 ❏	2 ❏	3 ❏	4 ❏	5 ❏
2. We also identify any specific technical skills each board member possesses and maintain a matrix of skills to ensure that we have the right mix of skills and avoid any skills gaps. (For example: Functional skills such as finance, human resources, legal, corporate social responsibility; as well as sector knowledge, international and relevant geographic experience.)	1 ❏	2 ❏	3 ❏	4 ❏	5 ❏
3. We have the necessary systems and procedures in place to improve the effectiveness of our board members and to remedy the situation, if and when a deficiency is identified. (For example: There is a regular board performance evaluation mechanism and a feedback mechanism to help improve board members' performance. We allocate resources to improve the skills of our board members. There is a clear system for renewal and succession planning of board membership.)	1 ❏	2 ❏	3 ❏	4 ❏	5 ❏
4. We have a competitive remuneration package that enables us to recruit the most appropriate independent members. (For example: We test the competitiveness of our remuneration package with market practices on a regular basis. We have not had any refusals by any candidate we approached. Current members are willing to provide sufficient time to board duties.)	1 ❏	2 ❏	3 ❏	4 ❏	5 ❏

(*Continued*)

Table 3.4 Continued

	Strongly Disagree	Disagree	Neutral	Agree	Strongly Agree
5. We have explicit conflict of interest and independence guidelines and we review these matters as they relate to each board member on a regular basis.	1 ☐	2 ☐	3 ☐	4 ☐	5 ☐
6. We have a full disclosure policy on board membership matters. (For example: We disclose the skills and experience of all board members, their remuneration, independence criteria, any decisions they have excused themselves from owing to any potential conflict of interest, their attendance record, and the nomination of any independent advisors in appropriate circumstances.)	1 ☐	2 ☐	3 ☐	4 ☐	5 ☐
7. The chairman of the board:					
a. Ensures that the board agenda contains items of relevance and value to directors and that the annual agenda covers all relevant dimensions	1 ☐	2 ☐	3 ☐	4 ☐	5 ☐
b. Ensures that board members are kept informed of the company's progress in implementing strategic decisions.	1 ☐	2 ☐	3 ☐	4 ☐	5 ☐
c. Allocates sufficient time during board meetings to discuss each item fully.	1 ☐	2 ☐	3 ☐	4 ☐	5 ☐
d. Ensures that issues are considered from different stakeholder perspectives and different angles prior to decision-making.	1 ☐	2 ☐	3 ☐	4 ☐	5 ☐
e. Encourages directors to ask questions and express their views at board meetings.	1 ☐	2 ☐	3 ☐	4 ☐	5 ☐
f. Ensures that the board comes to decisions once agenda items have been adequately discussed	1 ☐	2 ☐	3 ☐	4 ☐	5 ☐
g. Holds an in-camera session at the end of each board meeting to receive frank feedback from board members.	1 ☐	2 ☐	3 ☐	4 ☐	5 ☐
II. Do they function as an effective team?					
1. There is sufficient diversity of background between board members to ensure that different perspectives and skills are brought to bear on issues facing the company without creating an imbalance of perspectives or cliques. (For example: In such dimensions as risk vs. reward; short term vs. long term; effective oversight vs. motivating management; ethical considerations vs. market practices; and competing interests of different stakeholders, such as – shareholders, small and large; partners; management; employees; suppliers; dealers; customers; industry players; public administrators; and the community at large.)	1 ☐	2 ☐	3 ☐	4 ☐	5 ☐
2. There is mutual respect, trust, an open and transparent communication among board members.	1 ☐	2 ☐	3 ☐	4 ☐	5 ☐
3. The skill sets of board members complement each other and I believe that the risks that the company faces are better evaluated as a team.	1 ☐	2 ☐	3 ☐	4 ☐	5 ☐

(*Continued*)

Table 3.4 Continued

	Strongly Disagree	Disagree	Neutral	Agree	Strongly Agree
4. The board spends sufficient time together in plant and market visits as well as with operational managers to enable them to review the business informally and independently from the information provided at the board meetings.	1 ❑	2 ❑	3 ❑	4 ❑	5 ❑
5. Board committees:					
a. Current committee structure of the board is appropriate	1 ❑	2 ❑	3 ❑	4 ❑	5 ❑
b. The skills and talents of board members are well utilized in committee assignments	1 ❑	2 ❑	3 ❑	4 ❑	5 ❑
c. Committees are fulfilling their role to identify potential areas of improvement and to make recommendations to the board of directors to ensure that the company is run better. In particular there is no tendency to encroach on decision-making authority of either the management or the full board.	1 ❑	2 ❑	3 ❑	4 ❑	5 ❑
6. Audit committee: (Please answer d–g only if you are on the committee.)					
a. The charter, role and responsibilities are clear and appropriate.	1 ❑	2 ❑	3 ❑	4 ❑	5 ❑
b. Committee annual work plan and agendas are appropriate.	1 ❑	2 ❑	3 ❑	4 ❑	5 ❑
c. The composition of the committee is appropriate.	1 ❑	2 ❑	3 ❑	4 ❑	5 ❑
d. The committee is effectively chaired.	1 ❑	2 ❑	3 ❑	4 ❑	5 ❑
e. Information provided to the committee is relevant, comprehensive, timely and effectively presented, and enables effective monitoring.	1 ❑	2 ❑	3 ❑	4 ❑	5 ❑
f. Members of the committee are well prepared, informed, appropriately challenging and participate effectively.	1 ❑	2 ❑	3 ❑	4 ❑	5 ❑
g. An in-camera session is held separately with management, independent auditors and committee members to enable raising of relevant issues.	1 ❑	2 ❑	3 ❑	4 ❑	5 ❑
7. Nominating and corporate governance committee: (Please answer d–g only if you are on the committee.)					
a. The charter, role and responsibilities are clear and appropriate.	1 ❑	2 ❑	3 ❑	4 ❑	5 ❑
b. Committee annual work plan and agendas are appropriate.	1 ❑	2 ❑	3 ❑	4 ❑	5 ❑
c. The composition of the committee is appropriate.	1 ❑	2 ❑	3 ❑	4 ❑	5 ❑

(*Continued*)

Table 3.4 Continued

	Strongly Disagree	Disagree	Neutral	Agree	Strongly Agree
d. The committee is effectively chaired.	1 ☐	2 ☐	3 ☐	4 ☐	5 ☐
e. Information provided to the committee is relevant, comprehensive, timely and effectively presented, and enables effective monitoring.	1 ☐	2 ☐	3 ☐	4 ☐	5 ☐
f. Members of the committee are well prepared, informed, appropriately challenging and participate effectively.	1 ☐	2 ☐	3 ☐	4 ☐	5 ☐
g. An in-camera session is held to enable raising of relevant issues.	1 ☐	2 ☐	3 ☐	4 ☐	5 ☐
8. The compensation committee: (Please answer d–g only if you are on the committee.)					
a. The Charter, role and responsibilities are clear and appropriate.	1 ☐	2 ☐	3 ☐	4 ☐	5 ☐
b. Committee annual work plan and agendas are appropriate.	1 ☐	2 ☐	3 ☐	4 ☐	5 ☐
c. The composition of the committee is appropriate.	1 ☐	2 ☐	3 ☐	4 ☐	5 ☐
d. The committee is effectively chaired.	1 ☐	2 ☐	3 ☐	4 ☐	5 ☐
e. Information provided to the committee is relevant, comprehensive, timely and effectively presented, and enables effective monitoring.	1 ☐	2 ☐	3 ☐	4 ☐	5 ☐
f. Members of the committee are well prepared, informed, appropriately challenging and participate effectively.	1 ☐	2 ☐	3 ☐	4 ☐	5 ☐
g. An in-camera session is held to enable raising of relevant issues.	1 ☐	2 ☐	3 ☐	4 ☐	5 ☐
III. Do we have the right processes?					
1. The current numbers of board and committee meetings are adequate to keep the board members properly informed and involved.	1 ☐	2 ☐	3 ☐	4 ☐	5 ☐
2. The board meeting work plans and individual agendas are appropriate to address the key issues facing the company.	1 ☐	2 ☐	3 ☐	4 ☐	5 ☐
3. There is an explicit and adequate process to review and evaluate top management's performance.	1 ☐	2 ☐	3 ☐	4 ☐	5 ☐
4. There is an explicit and adequate process for succession planning, including development plans for senior management and monitoring progress as well as compensation policies to ensure the ability to attract and retain high quality management team.	1 ☐	2 ☐	3 ☐	4 ☐	5 ☐

(*Continued*)

Table 3.4 Continued

	Strongly Disagree	Disagree	Neutral	Agree	Strongly Agree
5. There is an explicit and adequate process for identifying the major risk areas (in strategic, operational, leadership, partnership, and reputation dimensions) and ensuring adequate mitigation strategies and systems are implemented.	1 ❏	2 ❏	3 ❏	4 ❏	5 ❏
6. The performance of the company with respect to its communication and disclosure policies with authorities, investors, analysts, and press is regularly reviewed by the board.	1 ❏	2 ❏	3 ❏	4 ❏	5 ❏
7. There is a board process to ensure that integrity of internal control and management information systems, including the assurance of the independence of the outside auditors and the availability of a fair and independent whistle-blowing process.	1 ❏	2 ❏	3 ❏	4 ❏	5 ❏
8. There is an explicit and adequate process to evaluate the effects of the company's business on different stakeholders and sustainability of the company's business.	1 ❏	2 ❏	3 ❏	4 ❏	5 ❏
9. There is an explicit and adequate investment evaluation and approval process; as well as a review of new market and product development activities.	1 ❏	2 ❏	3 ❏	4 ❏	5 ❏
10. There is an explicit and adequate self-evaluation process for the board covering the composition, processes, timely and relevant information availability, culture and climate, and learning for continuous improvement areas, and a feedback process.	1 ❏	2 ❏	3 ❏	4 ❏	5 ❏
IV. Do we have relevant and timely information?					
1. The pre-meeting papers are effective in helping the board members understand the issues and efficient in doing so.	1 ❏	2 ❏	3 ❏	4 ❏	5 ❏
2. The management keeps the board members informed of important matters between meetings.	1 ❏	2 ❏	3 ❏	4 ❏	5 ❏
3. Information provided to the board members:					
a. Gives an accurate and objective perspective.	1 ❏	2 ❏	3 ❏	4 ❏	5 ❏
b. Is timely for action	1 ❏	2 ❏	3 ❏	4 ❏	5 ❏
c. Enables effective monitoring.	1 ❏	2 ❏	3 ❏	4 ❏	5 ❏
d. Includes independent evaluations of market developments.	1 ❏	2 ❏	3 ❏	4 ❏	5 ❏
e. Includes relevant external and benchmark or competitive data.	1 ❏	2 ❏	3 ❏	4 ❏	5 ❏
f. Includes future perspective.	1 ❏	2 ❏	3 ❏	4 ❏	5 ❏
g. Includes potential impacts for different stakeholders.	1 ❏	2 ❏	3 ❏	4 ❏	5 ❏

(Continued)

Table 3.4 Continued

	Strongly Disagree	Disagree	Neutral	Agree	Strongly Agree
4. Where objectives or key performance indicators are not being met they are appropriately raised, remedial action plans made, and information provided for appropriate monitoring.	1 ☐	2 ☐	3 ☐	4 ☐	5 ☐
5. Ex-post evaluation of capital investments, acquisitions, and restructuring are provided with learning lessons.	1 ☐	2 ☐	3 ☐	4 ☐	5 ☐
6. The board reviews the disclosure policy on a regular basis and ensures strict adherence to it.	1 ☐	2 ☐	3 ☐	4 ☐	5 ☐
7. The board reviews the insider trading restrictions and ensures strict adherence to them. (There is an explicit policy document that is communicated with all relevant parties and posted in the company website; black-out periods are communicated with all insiders.)	1 ☐	2 ☐	3 ☐	4 ☐	5 ☐
V. Do we have the right culture?					
1. The atmosphere of the board is constructive and supportive.	1 ☐	2 ☐	3 ☐	4 ☐	5 ☐
2. The atmosphere is candid and open, encourages critical thinking and challenge.	1 ☐	2 ☐	3 ☐	4 ☐	5 ☐
3. There are no hidden agendas that impede the board's effectiveness and each director acts with integrity, basing each decision entirely on their belief in what is best for the company.	1 ☐	2 ☐	3 ☐	4 ☐	5 ☐
4. There is no discouragement for any director to press the management for a reconsideration, or for more information.	1 ☐	2 ☐	3 ☐	4 ☐	5 ☐
5. There is respect for management and each other, but each member exercises their own independent judgment without falling into "group thinking."	1 ☐	2 ☐	3 ☐	4 ☐	5 ☐
6. Each member comes to meetings well prepared and there is sufficient time for exchange of ideas and discussion.	1 ☐	2 ☐	3 ☐	4 ☐	5 ☐
7. Board discussions usually reach satisfactory closure.	1 ☐	2 ☐	3 ☐	4 ☐	5 ☐
VI. Are we providing the right kind of guidance?					
1. There is an effective strategic planning and review process in place.	1 ☐	2 ☐	3 ☐	4 ☐	5 ☐
2. The board has deep enough understanding of the capabilities of the company and the opportunities the company is facing to make informed strategic judgments.	1 ☐	2 ☐	3 ☐	4 ☐	5 ☐
3. The board has ample opportunity to influence strategy development.	1 ☐	2 ☐	3 ☐	4 ☐	5 ☐
4. The strategic plan has the right balance between short-term and long-term goals.	1 ☐	2 ☐	3 ☐	4 ☐	5 ☐

(Continued)

Table 3.4 Continued

	Strongly Disagree	Disagree	Neutral	Agree	Strongly Agree
5. The strategic plan has the right balance between the risks and potential rewards.	1 ❑	2 ❑	3 ❑	4 ❑	5 ❑
6. There is sufficient preparation and positioning to capture strategic opportunities.	1 ❑	2 ❑	3 ❑	4 ❑	5 ❑
7. The company has the capabilities and the resources to implement the approved strategy.	1 ❑	2 ❑	3 ❑	4 ❑	5 ❑
VII. Are we providing adequate oversight?					
1. There is an effective oversight and audit process in place.	1 ❑	2 ❑	3 ❑	4 ❑	5 ❑
2. The authority levels and approval mechanisms for decision-making are clearly established and only key strategic decisions are approved by the board.	1 ❑	2 ❑	3 ❑	4 ❑	5 ❑
3. There is an effective internal audit function covering financial, operational and compliance audits with the goal of bringing a systematic, disciplined approach to evaluate and improve the effectiveness of risk management, control, continuous monitoring, and governance processes.	1 ❑	2 ❑	3 ❑	4 ❑	5 ❑
4. Internal audit function works with the understanding of providing consultancy to management on ethical codes, potential conflict of interests, establishing control mechanisms when important projects are initiated and/or when the information systems are renewed.	1 ❑	2 ❑	3 ❑	4 ❑	5 ❑
5. Internal audit has direct access to the board for issues related to investigations of fraud, codes of conduct that are not consistent with ethical codes, and occasions where the top management is perceived not to act on time in high risk areas.	1 ❑	2 ❑	3 ❑	4 ❑	5 ❑
6. Crises management and business continuity plans are reviewed regularly and are adequate.	1 ❑	2 ❑	3 ❑	4 ❑	5 ❑
7. There are effective whistleblowing procedures.	1 ❑	2 ❑	3 ❑	4 ❑	5 ❑
Overall					
1. What are the top three key challenges facing the company?					
2. What was the board's most significant achievement last year, if any?					
3. What was the board's most notable shortcoming last year, if any?					
4. Do you have any specific recommendations to improve the board's effectiveness?					

Source: Corporate Governance – Self Evaluation Questionnaire by ARGE Consulting© based on the methodology explained in *ARGE Kurumsal Yönetişim Modeli* (ARGE Corporate Governance Model), ©ARGE, 2007.

and recommendations, sometimes with the help of outside advisors, to the full board and when appropriate to the general assembly.

The committee that handles the board compensation package has to focus on the following areas:

- The compensation package has to be competitive enough to attract appropriate members to join the board.

- The compensation package has to be flexible enough to be adjusted for market conditions.

- The incentives for board members should be aligned with the interests of the shareholders.

- The architecture must be transparent and easily understood by shareholders.

- Compensation packages vary by corporation and jurisdiction, but involve cash, shares, or options. It is preferable to tie board members' incentives to the long-term performance of the corporation rather than to short-term performance, as the main role of board members is to provide stewardship for the company.

One guideline for the value of director compensation that is utilized is to correlate it with the compensation of the CEO, normalized for time commitments. For example, if a director is expected to spend about 20 to 25 days annually on activities related to the company, then their pay should be about one-tenth of the CEO's, whose compensation is based on full-time commitment, or about 220 working days annually. However, in different jurisdictions different benchmarks may be utilized. It is best to use independent consultants to benchmark board members' pay with that in comparable companies in order to be able to attract and retain the best board members.

BOARD MEMBER DEVELOPMENT (ORIENTATION AND TRAINING)

In order to have meaningful discussions about real issues at board meetings, the members should have a similar level of understanding about the company, industry, and current market conditions that influence the key issues of the corporation. Therefore, new members should be brought up-to-date with a tailor-made orientation program. The orientation may be designed on behalf of the board by the corporate governance committee. The orientation may be conducted by the CEO, CFO, and human resources director, with respect to their relevant fields of expertise.

The orientation programs should be designed so that they are attended by the board members within their first few months of service and should acquaint them with the people, operations, customers, and main stakeholders of the company. For companies that have a wide geographic presence, opportunities have to be presented to the board members to visit critical locations. In as short a time as possible, new members should be informed of corporation strategies, financial results, reporting and internal control systems, critical policy areas such as human resources policies, and critical capabilities.

Apart from the orientation program, there should be a continuous development program for all directors, focusing particularly on technological, infrastructural, and regulatory developments critical for the company. Also, regular visits to key facilities and key markets are useful for gaining better understanding of the issues and the context.

The orientation program should include the following:

- The corporation's mission and vision.

- The corporation's strategies and goals.

- The corporation's products/services, strengths and weaknesses.

- The corporation's business processes, main customers, suppliers, and competitors.

- The corporation's business model, intellectual capital, and key assets.

- The corporation's organization, key executives, human resources systems, and key production facilities.

- Historically key events and developments for the corporation.

- The corporation's policies, ethics, internal controls, audit, accounting standards, and the regulations the corporation is subject to.

- The governance system and corporate culture.

- Information pertaining to the other board members and senior management.

"RIGHT PROCESSES" – SUMMARY

Processes are series of functions and actions to bring about a desired result. Processes are key to the execution of standards in a consistent manner. The corporate governance principles are useful only if applied consistently. Therefore, the board processes for selecting, developing, assigning responsibilities to, and evaluating the performance of its own members are key to ensuring that the board handles its main responsibilities of providing guidance and oversight adequately.

Consistency   Consistency in decisions and implementation can be achieved if every decision and action is tested by its conformity with the corporation's mission and vision.

Responsibility   Each employee of the corporation, irrespective of their title, should take responsibility for the work they do. This approach is vital to encouragement to take initiatives, to raising the level of knowledge, to gaining speed, and to the continuous development of the corporation's performance. The same holds for each board member.

Accountability   The board should base its decisions on verifiable, comparative data, and should ensure that this approach is propagated throughout the organization.

Fairness   Fairness in treating people is the most important feature in ensuring trust within the organization. Therefore, the way board decisions about performance are made and communicated is important.

Transparency   Providing up-to-date, relevant information to the board members improves board performance and increases trust to the management.

Effectiveness   The board's annual self-evaluation exercise is key to improving its effectiveness.

Deployment   Assigning certain functions to board committees helps in the more detailed consideration of key issues. It also helps the more effective utilization of specific skills of certain board members.

CHAPTER 4

Right Culture

The only man who makes no mistakes is the man who never does anything.

Teddy Roosevelt

MANAGING VS. PROVIDING GUIDANCE

A key to a successful board is a good understanding of the different roles of the management and the board. The board of directors is the **stewards of the corporation's assets**, tangible as well as intangible, and should **behave in such a manner as to create a climate for the sustainable success** and increase in value of the corporation. The board provides guidance and oversight to the management, and the management initiates and implements decisions. A board that interferes with management and assumes an operational role would in effect be a part of the management and therefore less independent from it. Such a board would therefore not be able to credibly exercise its control rights independently.

For board members, apart from independence, integrity, and leadership, the most important characteristic is a lack of ambition to replace the management with themselves. Only people content to serve in a secondary, behind-the-scenes role can have a productive and trusting relationship with the top management. The lack of rivalry fosters cooperation, eases the flow of information, and helps board members to serve as effective mentors.

The basic role of the board is to ensure that the corporation is led with an entrepreneurial spirit that enhances its value by **providing guidance** and **oversight**. Thus one of the key responsibilities of the board is the recruitment, appointment, evaluation, rewarding, and, when necessary, removal of the **CEO and top executives**. The board is also responsible for assessing and approving the **strategic direction** of the company, ensuring the **integrity of** all **public disclosures**, including financial and other stakeholder reporting, and also for ensuring that the management has instituted an **effective risk management** and **internal control system**. Finally, **monitoring performance** against agreed benchmarks, taking into account the competitive environment, is a key board responsibility.

The responsibility of the CEO is to be the executive leader. CEOs are responsible for enhancing the value of the corporation by leading the management team and the organization within the strategic direction approved by the board. In doing so they also ensure that not only the decision-making power at each level of management is not misused, but also that it is used with care and responsibility to meet stakeholder expectations. This kind of behavior is the essence of good corporate governance.

Corporate governance is **a culture, a climate,** and **a set of behaviors** that is exhibited throughout the organization, followed everywhere and every time, without written instruction or explicit mention. It is not a checklist or a chapter in a document, and is not limited to compliance.

Open-minded, early, and honest communication is a key enabler of a good governance culture. Transparency requires that analyses, decisions, and actions are documented, put into context, and considered for materiality. Information relevant for governance needs to focus on costs, risks, options, and impacts. Its context, timeliness, and comparison with relevant benchmarks are more important than its ultimate precision. Therefore, it is the management's responsibility to explain the bigger picture, issues, options, and recommendations in a way that is up-to-date and comprehensible, and in an executive format.

Professional diligence also requires that the management discloses mistakes, and problems without delay. This may be unpleasant, but it builds trust. If the management has valid concerns, the board has to know them. Mutual trust between the board and the management also requires the acceptance and the internalization of the separation of management and control rights. When the board challenges or rejects management's recommendations, it should not be taken as interference or as indicating a mistrust of management's competencies, but rather as an opportunity to integrate broader perspectives into corporate decision-making. It is the duty of the board to challenge, support, guide, and control the management. And it is the duty of the management both to initiate proposals and to implement what is ratified by the board in order to create value effectively.

IMPORTANCE OF BEHAVIORS IN ESTABLISHING A CULTURE

With the globalization of the world economy, both the size and the impact of many corporations are becoming greater than those of numerous national economies. Therefore, their responsibility extends not only to their shareholders, but also to numerous stakeholders throughout the globe. At the same time, as their value chains extend throughout the world, their dependence on others increases. Hence, the sustainability of a corporation becomes correspondingly dependent on their governance systems to ensure trust in their relations with their suppliers, employees, financial markets, governments, customers, and their communities.

Good corporate governance increases corporate value. Especially in emerging markets, there is a serious premium for good corporate governance. Governance ratings and rankings are only an inadequate proxy for measuring the effectiveness of governance. They are focused on easily observable characteristics, such as the separation of the chairperson's role from that of the CEO or the number of women on the board. Their focus is on inputs, not outputs. They do not link governance with company performance. They say nothing about the learning and development of governance. They do not attempt to measure the attitudes, behaviors, or climate of the board.

Good governance is a lot more than compliance. It is a culture and a climate of Consistency, Responsibility, Accountability, Fairness, Transparency, and Effectiveness that is deployed throughout the organization: the CRAFTED principles of governance.

The board's success depends on making sound judgments in numerous situations that involve balancing different interests:

- Risk vs. reward.

- Short term vs. long term.

- Effective oversight vs. motivating management.

- Ethical considerations vs. market practices.

- Competing interests of different stakeholders:

    ○ Shareholders, small and large.

    ○ Partners.

    ○ Management.

    ○ Employees.

    ○ Suppliers.

    ○ Dealers.

    ○ Customers.

    ○ Industry players.

    ○ Public administrators.

    ○ The community at large.

Success can be achieved in a sustainable basis only if the board behaves as a role model for implementing the CRAFTED principles of governance in its own operations, and ensures that the corporation follows these principles in making key decisions.

The tone at the top sets the corporate culture.[1] Therefore, not only the conduct of the board members but also their decisions and how they communicate these decisions are critical. All the members of the board should support, improve, and guide the corporate culture with their actions.

Corporate culture is the cornerstone of creating trust inside and outside the company. The implementation of CRAFTED governance principles, in all its activities, helps to increase both the trustworthiness and the value of the company. The most important role of the board is to increase the company's value by being fair and gaining the trust of all its stakeholders. A board that develops an appropriate corporate culture and structure, and ensure its sustainability, is more likely to achieve better and more sustainable business results. Such a culture becomes the corporate culture only when it is extended to everyone, and especially at the management levels of the corporation.

The following are important where corporate governance principles are to be deployed effectively:

- Identifying the decisions that require board approval.
- The decision-making processes of the board.
- Establishing the criteria and processes for selecting the board members and chairperson.
- Establishing a performance evaluation system for the board.

However, structural and procedural issues are not sufficient for good governance. Good governance needs people who understand the spirit of governance, internalize governance principles, and reflect them in all their actions.

The following are some examples of the types of behavior expected in a corporation that is governed well:

Examples of Behavior Expected in an Organization with Good Governance

1. Management should not benefit personally from the corporation's activities or assets, except from their stipulated compensation and reward packages.

2. There should be no transactions with the corporation or its affiliates that is not in line with market prices.

3. The management should not assume too much risk on behalf of the shareholders with the hope of inflating the short-term performance of the company.

4. The management should not use the corporate resources to build an empire for themselves.

5. There should be no tendency toward nepotism. Qualifications of the individuals should be the only criteria in selecting and promoting them.

6. Insider trading should be avoided.

7. There should be no hindrance to effective operation of internal control systems.

8. Management should assume the responsibility to ensure that all employees are adequately informed and trained to avoid any conflicts of interest with the corporation.

9. Management should see to it that all employees observe all legal and ethical stipulations, and that there is an effective whistleblowing mechanism to identify violations.

10. The independence of external auditors should not be endangered by giving them too many other assignments.

11. There should be a competitive compensation system to ensure that competent individuals with the right qualifications are attracted to the corporation and rewarded for performance.

12. No shareholder should be given preferential treatment, and commercial transactions made with shareholders should be conducted on an arm's-length basis.

13. Unethical conduct such as bribery should be a cause for dismissal.

14. Management must behave fairly towards all stakeholders, such as employees, suppliers, and distributors.

15. Overconfidence in internal capabilities has to be avoided, in order to be able to utilize third-party resources for improving the corporation's performance.

16. Reductions in investments to meet short term-goals should be avoided if they endanger the future of the company. In particular, investment in intangibles such as the brand has to be watched carefully, as it is difficult to measure the damage in the short term.

17. Continuous improvement and benchmarking with best-in-class examples should be encouraged.

18. Strict adherence to public disclosure requirements about developments that may have an effect on the value of the company should be observed.

19. Systematic assessment should be conducted of risks and opportunities concerning the corporation's future.

20. Corporate social responsibility toward society and future generations should be taken seriously.

CRITICAL THINKING SKILLS

Whenever everyone agrees with me, I always feel I must be wrong.

Oscar Wilde

It is very important that board members, when carrying out their responsibilities, possess a system of constructive critical thinking. One cannot expect a board to be successful if the members accept every proposal presented to them without evaluating it critically.

Critical thinking is challenging all assumptions, information and judgments, and evaluating different aspects of the issues at hand before coming to a conclusion. The goal is to form a solid judgment that reconciles evidence with common sense. Critical thinking involves making judgments about the relevance, significance, fairness, and logic of the issue at hand.

Individuals who possess critical thinking skills have the following characteristics:

- Systematic thinking and working discipline.

- Flexibility.

- Being open to new ideas and change.

- Integrity.

- Perseverance.

- Courage.

- Autonomy.

- Self-confidence.

A good critical thinker:

- Gathers and assesses relevant information.

- Thinks open-mindedly in considering alternative perspectives, recognizing and assessing their assumptions, implications, and practical consequences.

- Raises vital questions and problems, formulating them clearly and precisely.

- Comes to well-reasoned conclusions and solutions.

- Communicates effectively with others in figuring out solutions to a complex problem, without being unduly influenced by others' thinking on the topic.

A board member who is not well prepared before participating in a meeting cannot exercise the discipline that is required for critical thinking, nor can they win the other team members' trust. A board member who possesses critical thinking skills applies this skill not only to the issue at hand, but also to the board process for decision-making.

Anybody who does not have the humility to accept that his own views and approach could also be challenged by fellow board members cannot be a good board member. Such intolerance poisons the climate of the board.

Absence of critical thinking on the board results in unhealthy decisions. Therefore, one of the key responsibilities of the chairperson of the board is to encourage critical thinking and to create an environment conducive to challenge. The dimensions of critical thinking are as follows:

Dimensions of Critical Thinking

Critical thinking is:

- Being able to identify the relevant dimensions, being able to assign weights to each dimension, being able to identify which ones will have significance for the results, and being able to live with uncertainty about those which are not critical.

- Being able to identify information gaps that need to be remedied in order to solve the problem. Identifying ways to overcome information deficiency, and to raise questions to bootstrap the gaps in information.

- Having knowledge about theoretical models and being able to judge the information with respect to such models.

- Making sure that everybody understands the assumptions and theoretical underpinnings of such models.

- Being able to make inferences and checking what is presented for consistency.

- Being able to concur on objective criteria to judge alternatives.

- Being able to judge the strength, depth, and breadth of justifications for a decision.

POSITIVE AND CONSTRUCTIVE THINKING

You are what you think of. The rest is meat and bones. If you think of roses, you will become a rose garden, but if you think of thorns, you will become a thorn patch.

Mevlana

Life is a mirror. If you smile at it, it will smile back.

Just as critical thinking is important in reaching healthy decisions, positive and constructive thinking is the key to emotional intelligence, which promotes the participation and sharing of ideas and conclusions.

One of our social and undoubtedly flawed biases is the tendency to see each mistake as an opportunity to lay the blame for mistakes on others. This in turn causes people to hide mistakes, instead of utilizing them as an opportunity to learn. Innovation requires candor and the acceptance of mistakes. Mistakes are to be expected, not avoided. Each opportunity to learn is worth its weight in gold. Conducting an effective analysis of a failure requires self-confidence, a spirit of inquiry and openness, patience, and a tolerance for ambiguity. Success in innovation comes not with worries or withdrawal, but with the persistence, the perseverance, and the tenacity to continue until it works.

Creating an appropriate climate for learning is a critical leadership challenge. Actions speak louder than words. Therefore, leaders who wish to create an environment that promotes learning should start with themselves. They should share their own mistakes and the lessons they have learned in order to develop the feeling of trust within the corporation. They must further turn this into a common learning process and create a transparent environment that will set the stage for continuous learning. Leaders should ensure that the corporate culture embodies an understanding that "To win we have to make calculated experiments," rather than "We should do nothing for fear of making a mistake."

We must remember that in order to find the modern-day light bulb, Edison conducted thousands of unsuccessful experiments, looking at each one as a learning opportunity and never having lost his motivation. Anyone who wishes to improve the quality of life should first learn to think positively. This is because thought shapes belief, belief shapes behavior, and behavior shapes the results.

Those who are mentally healthy are also physically healthy. Consequently, positive thinking prolongs life and improves the quality of life.

The ability to think positively and constructively can be learned. In order to develop this skill, an effective first step is to learn from the experience of others. Therefore, identifying role models for positive and constructive thinkers could be a good starting-point from which to learn to do so. According to Dr Epstein,[2] such people:

1. Think in ways that make them less sensitive to disapproval and rejection.

2. Think in ways that facilitate effective action.

3. Focus their thoughts more on the task at hand and refuse to let their minds drift to unpleasant events of the past.

4. Think that failures are an important source of learning and refuse to equate failure with low self-worth; this approach saves them from wasting time and suffering psychological pain.

5. Do not classify others into "winners" and "losers," but accept people for who they are – as individuals.

6. Are optimists and able to see their actions and the world in a healthy and realistic perspective.

7. Welcome challenges with optimism and without fear and think constructively.

Positive and constructive thinking requires being at peace with oneself. Consistency of thought, expression, and behavior is the enabler of self-confidence, peace, and winning the trust of others.

The harshest form of criticism is often the kind we direct upon ourselves. No man is perfect, so instead of criticizing mistakes that are made, looking at them as an opportunity to learn will provide more constructive results. Positive thinking is not denying mistakes, but rather accepting them as opportunities to improve. It involves reviewing mistakes, devising ways to avoid them, and preventing their repetition.

If the board of directors takes a similar approach in dealing with the management, it will promote a climate of candor and corporate learning.

Trust is the key to positive and constructive thinking. Quality of life can be improved only by those who believe that they can manage change. Those who trust themselves and their colleagues are likely to improve the quality of life for all.

ESTABLISHING HIGH STANDARDS FOR HIGH PERFORMANCE

Performance is more than an outcome: it is a culture. Those corporations that realize lasting high performance have common features in their corporate culture. For example, the lasting position of General Electric among the top companies in the world is the result of such a winning culture. It is not a coincidence that GE alumni also perform well in other organizations.

One of the common characteristics of high-performance companies is their ability to take the initiative in creating new business models as well as implementing them in a disciplined manner.

Their management culture is shaped by remaining focused on producing results rather than excuses.

Another common characteristic of high-performance companies is the importance they place on recruiting, managing, and developing their human resources. In these companies senior management takes an active role in:

- The selection process of individuals.

- Their development.

- Creating opportunities for exposure to different experiences.

- Their compensation and reward.

- Providing encouragement to take initiatives.

This creates a culture of learning and continuous development. These companies not only employ such practices in their own organization, but also promote them throughout their value chain.

High-performance corporations also use technology and knowledge as a means to obtain a strategic advantage. IT investments are considered not only as a physical investment but also as a vehicle for changing the way they do business. Information systems are used in order to institutionalize competitive knowledge within the corporation.

Another common characteristic of such corporations is the careful attention paid toward performance management. Results are not the only thing considered in performance management; adherence to corporate values is also taken into consideration. Performance management systems include balanced, but focused, key performance indicators. They involve both internal and external indicators, as well as a development perspective. They set stretch targets. Every employee is expected to focus on the following three points in order to attain a culture of high performance:

1. Achieving business results.

2. Contributing to ensuring the continuous development of business processes.

3. Undertaking management initiatives for change in business models, markets, technologies, and products.

High performance can be achieved only through:

- Consistent leadership that has the ability to shape the corporate culture.

- Promoting continuous improvement and innovation.

- Developing people and network of relationships with a long-term and disciplined approach.

CODE OF CONDUCT AND ETHICS

If you don't want others to know about your sins, then don't sin at all.

Chinese proverb

Critical thinking, positive and constructive thinking, and asking for high standards are all approaches that must be embraced to increase the effectiveness of the board. However, the most important thing expected of the board is the responsibility for stewardship and the duty of care, which involves ensuring throughout the corporation a compliance with ethical rules above and beyond laws and regulations. Across the globe it is expected that corporations will take great care to exhibit the ethical behavior that provides them with the continuing social license to operate.

A corporation's reputation and even its livelihood are at great risk if the members cannot meet the expectations of the society through their behavior. The most basic responsibility of preventing moral weakness within a corporation belongs to its senior management. Tone at the top matters.

The following list outlines the inputs for the effective implemention of ethical standards:

Inputs for the Effective Implementation of Ethical Standards

- Tone at the top matters. The top management should be a role model with its behaviors adhering to the stated moral values of the corporation. No exceptions should be allowed, and all who demonstrate weakness in applying moral values should be punished swiftly.

- Ethical standards have to be documented and each employee provided with a copy to be signed on engagement. A document confirming conformity with the corporation's ethical values should be signed by all employees annually.

- Any violation should instigate a thorough investigation and actions should be taken against violators, consistently.

- Case studies of the implementation of ethical values should be a regular part of employee training programs.

- A thorough reference check should be conducted for every new employee, and any relationship with current employees should be documented.

- Any violation of ethical codes should be dealt with swiftly.

- A whistleblowing mechanism should be established and the confidentiality of whistleblowers should be protected.

- Social pressure and sanctions against whistleblowers should be avoided.

- Improvements to internal control mechanisms should be implemented when code violations are detected.

- Strict adherence to ethical codes should be a precondition for promotion.

When the subject in question is corporate morality, one of the most important points is the prevention of theft and fraud within a corporation and ensuring that employees do not put their own interests before the interests of the corporation they work for. In order to minimize such risks, corporations form internal audit and other control mechanisms. However, weaknesses that arise within the corporate culture may lead to weaknesses within these control mechanisms themselves. The board must take the necessary precautions to preserve the moral values within the corporation, identify principles and encourage these principles to be implemented.

Ethical values are perceived differently in different countries; however, on a global scale nine main themes appear, as follows:

- **Corporate social responsibility** A corporation is expected to contribute voluntarily to ensure a better environment and society. The expectation that it will respect human rights, institute healthy and safe working conditions, protect the environment, avoid being part of corruption, and meet international standards is not limited to the corporation's own organization, but extends also to the its suppliers and other business partners.

- **Fair investigation** A corporation is expected to be open and fair in sharing information and documents when it and/or its management is faced with any legal allegations, and not to attempt to hide or destroy any information. For example, the biggest blow to Arthur Andersen during the Enron incident came from not demonstrating the necessary sensitivity on this issue.

- **The responsibility to protect the environment** A corporation is expected to show the utmost care in not causing damage to the environment throughout its activities and the activities of its suppliers and business partners. Outsourcing certain activities does not exempt a corporation from upholding this responsibility.

- **Avoiding misrepresentation in public disclosures** A corporation's business results must be shared in a transparent manner. Not sharing them, or, even worse, presenting them in a misleading manner, is considered a grave error of judgment.

- **Effectiveness of internal controls** The senior management of a corporation is responsible for the effectiveness of internal controls to ensure that the employees obey the ethical standards. This responsibility encompasses agreements made with third parties, guarantees of the corporation's products and services rendered, and also financial transactions.

- **Consumer protection** Corporations blatantly violate ethical rules if they knowingly render services or present products that may harm or mislead their customers.

- **Unfair or deceptive competition** Among behaviors considered unacceptable are the following: marketing unwanted goods to customers, pressuring them to sign exclusivity agreements, and employing unaffordable pricing policies for a period of time with the hopes of doing away with the competition. Obvious transgressions in these areas may in fact be penalized by competition laws.

- **Preventing the exposure of unethical behavior** A corporation must make every attempt to prevent the use of the its resources by management to serve their own interests; if and when unethical behavior is discovered it must not prevent investigation by public prosecutors; and it must not protect those who exhibit unethical behavior.

- **The responsibility of the board** The board is responsible for the integrity of the corporation's public disclosures and for protecting the rights of its shareholders as a whole.

As the mutual interdependence of organizations increases globally, the value of being a trusted member of global networks increases as well. For example, an ISO certificate has become a prerequisite for exporting. Soon Basel II regulations for evaluating credit risk will become a standard for all small and large corporations. Even if corporate social responsibility has yet to become mandatory, initiatives like the United Nations Global Compact, will become indicators of being a reliable member of global networks. Therefore, monitoring initiatives such as these, contributing to their development, and incorporating the principles into business processes before they become mandatory, is great way to prepare for the future and become respected member of the global network.

Compliance with ethical standards is important in earning the trust of the community, local as well as global. Earning the trust of others creates value for the company.

"RIGHT CULTURE" – SUMMARY

Corporate culture is the key to creating a climate in which a set of desired behaviors flourish in the organization. Tone at the top, starting with the choice of the CEO and top management, as well as the behavior of the board, is key to establishing "the right culture."

Corporate governance is a culture, a climate, and a set of behaviors promoting consistency, responsibility, accountability, fairness, transparency, and effectiveness that is deployed throughout the organization. It is the responsibility of the board to ensure that these principles are followed everywhere and every time so as to guarantee that the decision-making power at each level of management not only is not misused but also is used with care and responsibility to meet stakeholder expectations.

Such an effort involves the corporation not only having the right people, right processes, and right control mechanisms, but also those who head it providing a role model with their own behavior. In short, good corporate governance is a culture that earns the corporation the trust of all its stakeholders to ensure that they will continue to invest time and resources for sustainable success.

Consistency Corporate governance means being trusted by all stakeholders. Any behavior that is in conflict with the corporate governance principles would render claims for corporate values meaningless. Therefore, consistency of values, communications, and actions is key to earning trust.

Responsibility It is important that board members assume the responsibility to demonstrate an understanding of critical thinking and expect high standards of performance and ethical behavior.

Accountability In order to earn the trust of stakeholders, the necessary precautions should be taken to ensure the timeliness and integrity of public disclosures.

Fairness If a corporation is to increase its value by the alignment of the interests of its stakeholders with its own, the way all stakeholders are treated needs to be fair. Exhibiting positive and constructive thinking improves the perception of fairness by stakeholders.

Transparency In order for the feeling of trust to develop within a corporation, the mistakes should be shared openly and treated as a common learning opportunity. Transparency means that each decision can be supported by adequate analysis.

Effectiveness Effectiveness of governance requires that management rights to initiate and implement are separated from the control rights to approve and monitor, as well as to take action to evaluate, reward, or remove those who carry the management rights.

Deployment Corporate governance is not just for the board of directors. It affects everybody within an organization. Any person representing or making corporate decisions has to be part of the governance system that ensures the effectiveness of control systems.

Positive, constructive, and critical thinking; taking up the challenge to reach stretch targets; and the internalization of ethical behavior are the basic elements of governance culture.

NOTES

1 In the words of Mervyn E. King, the chairman of the Global Reporting Initiative, "Tone at the top sets the tune in the middle."
2 Seymour Epstein, *Constructive Thinking: The Key to Emotional Intelligence*, Greenwood, 1998.

CHAPTER 5

Right Information

Time stays long enough for anyone who will use it.

Leonardo da Vinci

BOARD INFORMATION

In order for the board of directors of a corporation to be effective, balanced information regarding the corporation must be shared with all the members systematically and in a timely manner. Balance refers not only to the different dimensions of information, but also to its detail. Relevance and context are two key elements for board information.

Putting information into context requires an ability to show the bigger picture as well as including comparative benchmarking data. Relevance of information, in turn, is related to the decision-making process. The board has to understand the issue, and the options, costs, risks, and impacts of each option for different stakeholders.

It is recommended to have an annual board schedule and agenda, in order to facilitate the preparation of board information on a timely basis. However, as the issues facing the corporation change, so do the information needs of the board. Providing the board with necessary and sufficient information to facilitate decision-making is a challenging and dynamic task. It is good practice to establish a process of reviewing regularly how satisfied the board is with the information presented. Such a review should cover the following subjects:

- What information the board needs to do its job.

- How often it wants this information.

- The format of the information to be presented.

Given this board feedback, the management can establish the content, format, and frequency of information to be provided to the board.

However, the systematic sharing of information with board members should not prevent them from requesting additional information. The request for additional information may stem from the fact that insufficient information has been presented to reach a decision, or the validity of the information may be questioned. Such skepticism is often useful, especially when new, risky avenues are being considered, and when competitors' moves do not fit the current mental models.

A board's most valuable resource is time. Hence, reports presented to the board should be clearly identified as to whether they are intended for monitoring, decision-making or informative purposes, and provided in a timely fashion to enable adequate review.

Successful corporate governance requires assessments that rely upon current and reliable information. Just as any living organization that is not fed properly cannot thrive, one cannot expect a board that is not adequately informed to reach healthy conclusions. Consequently, the scope and quality of information presented to a board is a critical factor in determining the quality of its corporate governance.

The choice of subjects the board is informed about and the detail of the information presented depend on issues the corporation is faced with, which may differ from one corporation to another or differ within the corporation itself from time to time. However, the information presented to the board may be summarized under the following headings:

- Information required to support board decisions, particularly investment and strategic issues.

- Information about industry trends, developments, and the company's positioning.

- Information that will allow a sound assessment of risks the corporation may face.

- Information necessary to assess the corporation's performance.

- Legal and regulatory developments and compliance issues.

- Information related to developments with stakeholders, and relationships with them.

Aside from developments related to a corporation's performance and its strategic projects, the board need to be up-to-date on the following issues:

- Competitors, customers, main suppliers, substitute product markets.

- General, social, economic, environmental, political, and technological developments.

- Regulatory changes.

- Changes in market conditions.

- Mergers and acquisitions developments in the industry.

- Share performance and the expectations of shareholders.

- Employee and customer satisfaction surveys.

- Developments in the company's intellectual capital assets.

Therefore, the board information system should incorporate these matters in a systematic fashion, but prioritize them according to their relevance for decision-making.

The board has the duty to ensure the integrity of the public disclosures of the company. Therefore, information about the internal control systems should also be made available to the board. In addition, the internal audit department and the external auditors should have direct access to the board so as to inform it of any internal control weaknesses. Finally, the board should have direct access to whistle-blowing activities and procedures in order to be aware of code violations immediately.

Another key responsibility of the board is to ensure that the company has a properly functioning risk management system. Therefore, the board should be informed about the way risks are identified, managed, and mitigated by the management. Risk management strategies for major corporate risks should be approved by the board.

The board is responsible also for ensuring that an effective succession plan is ready for implementation. It therefore should have sufficient information about key potentials within and outside the company and about their competencies, experiences, and performance. The development plan for key executives should also be part of the board information package. In addition, the board members should have access to key executives during various board activities in order to be able to evaluate their potential.

Board members must be allowed ample time to review and study the information presented to them before meetings; meeting agendas must be comprised of the most important issues that the corporation is faced with; and sufficient time must be set aside to allow for adequate discussion of critical issues. This should increase the effectiveness of board meetings as a discussion and joint decision-making platform, as opposed to one-sided information-loading by the management. Issues such as strategic assessments, risk assessments, and continuity plans, which may need additional discussion, may be handled in special retreats so as to provide sufficient time for discussion.

In addition, the board should hold in-camera sessions without the executives in order to be able to raise and discuss confidential matters. The board members should also have access to independent advisors whenever they deem it necessary, in order to get third-party opinions on critical issues.

The principal desirable qualities of board information may be summarized as follows:

Characteristics of Board Information

- One of the key constraints of board members is time. Therefore, the board information package should include only necessary and sufficient information, in a concise manner.

- In order to be meaningful, board information has to include comparisons with budgets, past performance, and industry benchmarks.

- Board information has to be current and presented in a timely fashion to enable the members to digest it.

- The information has to support decision-making by including the alternatives, costs, benefits, risks, and impacts on different stakeholders.

- The information should not be misleading and should be derived from the best available, verifiable sources.

- Presentation of the information has to be simple and easy to understand in order to enable the members to focus on the content, rather than having to try to decipher it.

- The theoretical models that the information is based on, and the main assumptions, should be clearly identified for more effective evaluation.

LEAD INDICATORS

One issue the board should be aware of is that the information presented to them is generally based on past performance. Also, performance indicators that are easier to measure get precedence. However, most of the board decisions are made for the future, so, access to lead indicators is important.

Companies who do not pay sufficient attention to lead indicators generally do not realize serious problems until it is too late. Therefore, the attention that management and board pay to lead indicators should be just as careful as that which they pay to business results. For example, a decline in customer satisfaction today may be an indicator of a decline in profits in the future. A decline in market share in a particular niche may be an indicator of the diminishing innovation capability of the company.

Customer complaints are also an important lead indicator. Failing to learn from them may cause bigger problems in the future. Focusing only on results and not paying sufficient attention to organizational process, and infrastructural developments may result in the repetition of mistakes. Therefore, customer complaints should not only be dealt with swiftly to increase customer satisfaction, but also be used to identify and remedy root causes.

The onset of problems in most corporations is due to not being perceptive of change. Thus, for example, Xerox, who failed to realize the importance of their own innovations, missed a significant opportunity in the personal computer revolution. Therefore, indicators such as the proportion of income coming from products and/or services introduced in the last few years should be watched carefully.

Similarly, performance in new markets should also receive special attention. When a board does not fully understand the competitive dynamics of a new market, errors of judgment, leading to too much or too little investment, are easily made.

Understanding the source of an increase or a decrease in profits, and variance analyses of past performances or budgets, are also key indicators of potential problems. For example, if a significant part of a financial institution's profit comes from trading activities, the board should make itself comfortable about the trading risks the company assumes. Similarly, if the source of profits is the value increase in inventories, due to events such as commodity price variations, then the company should be prepared financially for the reverse trends. Otherwise, as the market trends turn, the whole institution may be at risk.

Another warning for the board would be a tendency of top management to silence people with opposing views. For example, mega investments should be carefully watched for both schedule slippages and cost overruns. The sooner the board know about any potential problem, the better the solutions will be. Emotional attachment to such projects by the management should be avoided. With a system based upon transparency and objective data, it is possible to overcome such problems before they get out of hand.

Any indication of overconfidence on the part of the management or of underestimating the competition is another sign that needs to be watched by the board. Management that does not pay sufficient attention to relations with competitors, suppliers, and distribution channels may be drawing upon the goodwill account of the company. Therefore, independent stakeholder satisfaction surveys should be shared with the board for early warning signs.

In short, lead indicators such as perception, satisfaction, learning and innovation, which are relatively harder to measure, should be among the performance measures regularly reported to the board. Paying attention to such lead indicators is good practice for risk management. One example of a lead indicator is the Turkish Customer Satisfaction Index:

A Lead Indicator: The National Turkish Customer Satisfaction Index

Customer satisfaction surveys are important lead indicators for companies. Future success is a function of customer loyalty. This is the reason why KalDer, who promotes improving management quality in Turkey, has undertaken to conduct customer satisfaction surveys for key industries in Turkey and to share the index based on these studies publicly. The National Quality Movement, initiated by KalDer about 10 years ago while I served as the chairman, has been instrumental in developing numerous world-class applications of the EFQM (European Foundation for Quality Management) model. Over this period, Turkey has become one of the top two countries in terms of having European Quality Awards Winners. In developing and publicizing the Turkish Customer Satisfaction Index (TCSI), KalDer now aims to encourage replication of these successful examples throughout different industries. The methodology of TCSI is based on the ACSI – American Customer Satisfaction Index – with project management support of from the University of Michigan Stephen M. Ross Business School and the National Quality Research Center (NQRC), and is applied in numerous countries.

TCSI is based on an econometric model and provides information about trends in customer satisfaction, and loyalty and their potential impact on the competitiveness of the companies in numerous industries. One of the key strengths of TCSI is its ability to benchmark performance within and between industries and countries. It covers both the private sector as well as the public sector. This kind of comparable data based on a common methodology are valuable for investors, managers, and board members, as well as customers. Thus, KalDer is using the power of information about lead indicators to help companies improve their management quality.

It is not that difficult to identify potential problems. Just like individuals, companies have to have regular checkups to identify potential weaknesses, and need to take measures to overcome them; hence the Argenti Method:

The Argenti Method

Companies fail when the management and board are unable to identify the industry trends and developments within the organization. John Argenti devised a simple methodology which enables management to conduct a self-evaluation that predicts company failures with great precision. This methodology is focused on three basic areas:

- Structural issues:
  - Despotic management that discourages bad news.
  - Not separating management rights and control rights, such as for example having the CEO and the chairman as the same person.
  - Not having sufficient numbers of active independent board members.
  - Not having sufficient diversity at the board and at the top management team.
  - Having a weak chief financial officer.
  - Lack of depth in the management team.
  - Lack of succession planning.
  - Lack of budget discipline and internal control systems.
  - Deficiencies in cost accounting and cost management.
  - Having a slow response rate to market developments.
- Major mistakes:
  - High debt/equity ratio.
  - Too fast growth.
  - Undertaking an investment which is too large for the company.
- Incongruence of objectives and resources:
  - Creative accounting practices.
  - Decline in employee and customer satisfaction indices.
  - Deterioration of other financial indicators.

See John Argenti, *Corporate Collapse: Causes and Symptoms*, McGraw-Hill, 1976.

REPORTING PERFORMANCE

Performance that is not measured cannot be improved.

Performance reports are critical inputs for both board and management. The effectiveness of the board increases with the quality of information provided to it. When there is no information, prejudices take precedence and improving management quality becomes difficult. Also, in order to be able serve as a trusted member of a global network, a company has to share performance information with others. For example, in order to access equity markets so as to undertake bigger projects, they have to fulfill the public disclosure requirements of capital market regulatory agencies. In order to be able to export, they have to have current ISO certification.

In many organizations, the board information package is based on tax or regulatory reporting requirements, or special requests are fulfilled on an ad-hoc basis. However, corporate information systems should regularly be utilized to manage and report performance in comparison with budgets, past performance, and competitive benchmarks. Corporate databases should include all the information necessary for leading, managing, and controlling the corporation.

For corporate information to possess integrity all the primary data must be verifiable and comparable with both past data and other industry benchmarks. This also gives assurance to the board that further detailed analyses could be conducted to identify the root causes of issues. Therefore, ensuring the integrity of data is among the key responsibilities of the internal audit function.

The extent to which corporate information systems produce current and up-to-date information is an important consideration for decision-making. Hence investing in consolidation processes to produce performance reports from transaction-level data increases the effectiveness of decision-making.

The content and coverage of the performance reports need to address every aspect of corporate performance, such as the measures related to the efficiency of input utilization, the effectiveness of results, and also the development of assets both tangible and intangible.

Performance reports should also include the management's projections and assessments of potential risks. Developments at competitors, and market developments, as well as the management's evaluation of such developments, increase the value of performance reports. Such evaluations also provide input to the board about the management's readiness.

Performance is a relative measure. It needs a context, both internal and external. Therefore, performance measurements should always be benchmarked against previous performances, budgets, plans, and competitors.

MANAGING UNCERTAINTY

The quality of the process by which the decisions are made is just as important as the quality of information feeding into this process:

The Decision-Making Process

- Good decisions are based on good questions. The level of questioning must be properly balanced not to eliminate the alternatives without evaluating them properly.

- Criteria for evaluation should be determined prior to decision-making.

- Creating as many alternatives as possible improves the quality of decision-making. The identification of alternatives requires creativity.

- Good decisions also need well-established priorities, because most tough decisions require making a choice among alternatives none of which produces the best result in every dimension.

- Decision-makers have to thoroughly understand the risks and consequences of every alternative in order to make informed judgments.

- In many cases uncertainties regarding the consequences of alternatives cannot be resolved fully. Therefore, making assessments about probabilities is a key decision-making competency.

- Whenever uncertainties remain, decisions may not produce the expected outcomes. Therefore, the acceptance level for undesired outcomes should also be determined prior to decision-making.

- The potential effects of current decisions on future decisions should also be evaluated. Today's decisions not only may limit tomorrow's alternatives, but also may influence the future decisions of others who observe our current decisions.

- These principles do not guarantee good decisions, but they do help to minimize decision stress.

Decisions affect the development of people, institutions, and countries. Every day, every one of us, on behalf of ourselves and on behalf of our corporations, and some of us on behalf of our countries, is making decisions. Some of these decisions are easy, while others are difficult.

Certain principles guide good decision-making processes.

First of all, the board should evaluate the issue to identify whether or not it is important or urgent and requires a board decision. Making such an evaluation is critical to focussing on a limited number of vital issues and not taking management's place. Then the facts related to the issue, as presented by the management, should be evaluated in order to understand the situation thoroughly. The data and analyses presented should address any remaining uncertainties and allow judgments to be made about them.

The second step in board decision-making is ensuring that the alternatives presented by the management are comprehensive and that their costs, benefits, risks, and impacts are well understood. Often, decisions have to be made before all the uncertainties are resolved. When uncertainty cannot be reduced it has to be embraced and managed. From a managerial perspective there are four categories of uncertainty:

1. Distinct variability.

2. Foreseeable uncertainty.

3. Unforeseeable uncertainty.

4. Chaos.

Each requires a different approach to manage.

A variability due to a number of small effects that are difficult to control is generally managed using statistical control methods. The root causes of this type of variability are identified, variability is reduced, and the remaining variability is managed by allocating extra resources. One example is having work-in-progress inventories in order to manage manufacturing variability in different stations.

The second type of uncertainty is where potential outcomes are known, but not the probability of their occurrence. Foreseeable uncertainty can be managed by utilizing "decision trees." Once each potential path is identified, the management can identify action plans to be implemented under different outcomes and can also devise strategies to influence the probability of the occurrence of certain paths. Such contingency plans and strategies to reduce risks by cooperating with third parties are among the measures that could be taken to manage foreseeable uncertainties.

With the third type of uncertainty, the unforeseeable kind, the number of potential paths and outcomes are too numerous to be handled by decision trees. In this situation, the most effective methodology to utilize is scenario analysis. Scenario analysis is a process of analyzing possible future events by considering alternative possible outcomes. The analysis is designed to allow improved decision-making by allowing the consideration of outcomes and their implications. Scenarios are prepared for certain "typical" outcomes, and risk mitigation strategies for these cases are discussed within the management team for mental preparation. Scenarios encourage creativity. Scenario analysis also allows for testing the flexibility and the adequacy of adopted strategies under different conditions. Scenario analysis also speeds up the process of corporate learning.

The fourth and last type of uncertainty, chaos, is usually faced only for a limited period of time. In this type of uncertainty, where risks are at their peak, those players who have sufficient resources can utilize them to shape the future according to their preferences.

In order to manage uncertainty, a board may need different tools to increase their understanding of potential uncertainties. Once uncertainties are properly evaluated, they can be managed, and choice among alternatives can be made based on their costs, benefits, and risks. Finally, decisions have to be explained to those involved and affected, and followed up to ensure proper and effective implementation.

"RIGHT INFORMATION" – SUMMARY

The quality of board decision-making is a function of the quality of information supplied to the board. Establishing and maintaining a board information system is the joint responsibility of the chairperson, the board members, the CEO, and the staff members who work with the board.

Consistency   Consistency is a key test of information quality.

Responsibility   The responsibility of the board is to request, and that of the management to provide, information that would enable the members to exercise informed judgments about every significant and relevant risk and option for the corporation.

Accountability   The sincerity, accuracy, and authenticity of information of information provided to the board is an indicator of a management culture of accountability. This culture is enhanced by internal control mechanisms.

Fairness   Adequate preparation by board members is a requirement for the fair utilization of board information.

Transparency   Transparent and data-based information flow will ensure that healthy decisions are made by the board.

Effectiveness   Better information flow to the board is the critical link between informed directors and effective oversight. A good indication of good governance is when board members are not surprised.

Deployment   To the extent that the information requested by the board is also utilized by the management to ensure the justification of management decisions, the deployment of a successful management information system may be said to have been accomplished.

CHAPTER 6

Right Guidance

Vision without action is a daydream. Action without vision is a nightmare.

Japanese proverb

The board of directors is responsible for the key strategic direction of the company, ensuring that the right management team is in place to implement the strategy, to evaluate and reward the management's performance, and to ensure that the company has an effective internal controls and audit system.

The role of the board is to provide strategic guidance and oversight to ensure value creation.

STRATEGIC GUIDANCE

Concept of Strategy

In strategy it is important to see distant things as if they were close and to take a distanced view of close things.

Miyamoto Musashi

Success is sustainable "value creation." Sustainability in value creation requires not only "doing the right things" (strategy) and "doing things right" (total quality management), but also having the "right structure and culture" (good governance).

Compliance is a necessary condition for a good board, but definitely not a sufficient one. A board is also required to challenge, shape, and approve the strategy of the corporation.

"Strategy" comes from the Greek word *stratēgos*, which derives from two Ancient Greek words, *stratos* (army) and *ago* (I lead).

Strategic thinking is the ability to differentiate on a consistent manner. "Me-too" strategies do not create sustainable value.

In order for a board to contribute meaningfully to the strategic vision of the company, the members need to have the following:

- A good understanding of the industry, the competition, and the context.

- Experience in setting and implementing strategy.

- The commitment to demonstrate critical thinking skills.

The essence of strategy is to make consistent choices on which demand (current or potential) to fulfill, and how. What differentiates a company is its mission, vision, and the strategy it follows to reach them.

Companies that have a clear mission, vision, and strategy:

- Benefit by focusing their resources, physical and mental, and avoid activities that do not create value.

- Create a better balance between short-term and long-term goals.

- Benefit by having a tool for team-building and the motivation for more effective resource utilization.

- Capture potential value creation opportunities faster.

In short, luck favors prepared minds.

Effective communication of the mission and vision of the company also improves the effectiveness of their implementation. While the approval of the mission, vision, and strategies is a board responsibility, the responsibility for their implementation belongs to the management.

An Effective Vision Is

- *Vividly imaginable*: Provides a picture of success for the future.

- *Desirable*: Responds to the expectations of all stakeholders.

- *Stretched but realistic*: Sets a goal that is feasible to achieve with hard work.

- *Focused*: Clear enough to provide guidance in decision-making.

- *Flexible*: Easy to adapt for changing conditions and different dimensions.

- *Easy to communicate*: So that all employees can understand and internalize.

Setting the strategy is an analytically oriented art. The primary purpose of strategic planning is to build "prepared minds." If the key decision-makers have a solid understanding of the business, its strategy, and the assumptions behind that strategy, they will be able to respond swiftly to the challenges and opportunities as they occur. A good strategy is like a compass. It helps in guiding the company through the difficulties of the marketplace. Devising the strategy is the responsibility of the management. However, in challenging, shaping, and approving the strategy the board should evaluate it from the following perspectives:

- **Fit between strategy and resources** One perspective to question is whether the strategy is in congruence with the organization's competencies, structure, culture, reward mechanisms, and processes, and with the resources it can mobilize.

- **Clarity of focus** One of the key aspects of strategy is making a choice. Therefore, identifying what not to do is just as important is identifying what to do.

- **Dynamic** A strategic plan should take into account the potential responses of all relevant parties, competitors, suppliers, customers and so on. A good plan should also include contingency plans for the expected responses of various stakeholders.

- **Holistic** The implications of implementing the strategy for all the key functions should be thought out.

For Effective Communication a Vision Statement Should

- Be easy to understand and remember, clear, and lean.

- Be enriched by examples and stories for ease of recall.

- Be communicated consistently through different media to increase mind share.

- Have linkages between the key decisions and the vision provided.

- Have leaders who practice what they preach. **Actions speak louder than words**.

- Receive feedback, since two-way communication produces enrichment.

Key areas where the strategy should be questioned are:

- How to satisfy the customers.

- How to grow the business.

- How to respond to the changing conditions and trends.

- How to improve innovativeness and capture opportunities.

- How to manage the threats and risks.

Implementing a strategy requires discipline, in strategic thinking as well as in execution. However, although it is often suggested, the assumption of superior execution is not a strategy.

In defining the strategy, three dimensions have to be identified: (1) strategic intent, (2) strategic geography, and (3) strategic approach.

- According to strategy guru Michael Porter there are three generic strategies:

  ○ Being the lowest-cost competitor.

  ○ Providing a differentiated product or service to receive a better price.

  ○ Focusing on a niche market, and trying to be the lowest-cost competitor or providing differentiated products or service for that niche.

- Strategic geography refers not only to the physical geography of operations, but also to the choice of products and services, as well as to the choice of which part of the value chain to focus on and how to organize the rest of the value chain.

- Strategic approach refers to the choice of organic growth, inorganic growth, or business partnerships. Hence, the board should be interested not only in the markets the company operates in, but also in the market for companies in relevant industries.

In order to create value, companies need to identify unfulfilled demand areas. At the same time they have to mobilize resources to satisfy this demand.

There are six different dimensions of capital to mobilize in order to create value. Therefore, it is important to identify parameters to measure and develop resources in every dimension.

Six Dimensions of Capital

- *Financial assets*: Relate not only to what is available in the balance sheet, such as cash, receivables, and so on, but also to the cash generation capacity of the company as well as to the access of the company to equity and debt markets.

- *Physical assets*: Relate to land, buildings, or equipment.

- *Intangible assets*: Relate to rights and options of the company such as copyrights, trademarks, and patents.

- *Human capital*: Relates to the knowledge, skills, and competencies of the human resources. Therefore, is a function of the ability of the company to keep its human resources.

- *Relationship capital*: Relates to the value of customers, brand, and networks with stakeholders in the value chain.

- *Structural capital*: Relates to the organizational structure, processes, and databases of the company.

Sometimes more value may be created by selling these assets rather than utilizing them operationally.

Developing a Strategy Culture

Strategic planning is the responsibility of top management, who are also responsible for implementing the strategy. It cannot be delegated to a strategic planning department. This is particularly so because the most important benefit of the strategic planning process is the mental preparation it provides for the managers who are involved in the strategic planning process.

While the formal annual planning process must ultimately be owned and driven by the CEO, it is the strategic planning department that plays an important role as the internal consultant who helps to identify critical issues, collects information from the fringes of the organization to identify trends and critical changes in the context, and designs and runs the process where the top management considers strategic options and their risks and resource requirements.

A typical strategic planning department consists of a small number of high-quality people, rising stars from operational units. Generally, this staff is also utilized for executing special projects, and for preparing for analyst meetings and board meetings.

It is recommended that the board allocate a separate annual meeting to review, challenge, and approve the strategy for the corporation. In order to create a strategy culture within the organization:

- The mission and vision of the company has to be shared openly with all employees and stakeholders. This helps in clarifying the expectations of all the stakeholders and mobilizing resources toward a common goal.

- Organizational structure and processes have to be adjusted to deliver the strategy.

- Education and training should be provided in order to improve organizational capabilities and competencies. Improving the skills of the employees enables them to be empowered to deliver the strategy.

- Steps should be taken to ensure that business systems in all functional areas such as human resources and management information systems are aligned with the strategy. This is critical in achieving successful implementation.

- Key performance indicators and reward mechanisms should be aligned with the strategy. This is essential in motivating the whole system to deliver the strategy.

The mental preparation of the management team is the key benefit of the strategic planning process. When all the members of the top management understand the strategic choices, the underlying assumptions, the linkages between them, and the risks they incur, then when conditions change they can make the necessary adjustments coherently and on time. Moreover, and perhaps more importantly, such mental preparation helps them influence the conditions in their favor.

The essence of strategy is choice. **Making a choice is inherently risky**. The background, experience, and interests of those involved in the strategy development process influence their choices. One of the key issues that the board has to consider is ensuring that the rewards for the management are aligned with the strategy. Another key area is the alignment of the competencies of the management team with the strategy.

For example, if there are frequent changes in management teams then the managers may be focused on short-term returns and ignore long-term competency development issues. Hence many boards prefer to provide rewards that are based on long-term value creation. Balanced scorecards are also useful tools for providing multidimensional performance targets.

Also, it is important to watch for the congruence of the risk profiles of the company and the management. For example, top managers who are coming close to retirement age tend to be more conservative. On the other hand, especially in bull markets, managements tend to assume significant risks in order to provide better short-term relative performance.

Another risk area arises from groupthink. Especially when the management team have similar backgrounds, their blind spots may be common as well. New businesses or new geographies may require a different set of skills from those that brought previous success. Therefore, while decision-making for small investments could be delegated, significant decisions that have significant potential impact on the company's future should be considered with extra care. Large corporate transactions are among such issues.

The challenging of strategic choices by the board should not be seen by the management as revealing a lack of confidence. A healthy culture of challenge is important to ensure that all risk areas are identified and that alternatives are developed for strategic choices. The chairperson of the board has a critical role in creating such a climate in the boardroom.

Obviously, strategy-making is as much an art as it is an analytical process. However, to the extent that strategic alternatives are evaluated based on concrete data, it would be easier to come to a common conclusion. Also, strategy-making is an iterative process. Therefore, once an approach is developed and deployed, it is important to measure and review the results, and to make assessments for further modifications.

In short, understanding, challenging, shaping, and approving strategy is a key board responsibility. Therefore, board members have to have the competencies, the industry savvy, and the time commitment to be able to provide strategic guidance and to ensure that the company is led in a strategic direction that is likely to create and capture value.

Understanding Statistics

Having a good understanding of statistics is important in evaluating data. While it is better to base decisions on data, it is important to remember that statistics may be misleading. One of the key issues to watch out for is the way data are collected. For example, if a pilot study is based on current customer lists, then there will be a selection bias, as those who chose competitors will not have been considered. Another key issue arises from extreme data points. For example, the mean of a sample may be unduly influenced by a few outliers. Therefore, it is important to evaluate the accuracy and representativeness of outliers.

Also, correlation does not imply causality. Therefore, one has to ask three questions:

1. Is there a theoretical model which suggests causality?

2. Which variables are the independent variables and which is the dependent variable?

3. Could there be any other explanation for the correlation? For example, a correlation between an increase in egg prices and atmospheric temperature does not imply that increasing egg prices would have an effect on the climate!

Statistics reduce uncertainties about predictions. However, unlike mathematics, statistics do not prove a hypothesis or refute it with certainty; they just provide a confidence interval. Therefore, statistically it may not be possible to differentiate between a 4 and a 5 in a sample with a standard deviation of 2. While statistics can be a very useful tool, we have to be very careful in making statistical deductions.

Portfolio Strategy

As the globalization of capital flows and commerce increases, so does competition. Boards therefore are faced increasingly with choices about where to compete. Managing the portfolio of businesses becomes a key interest area for a board. They need to decide where to focus investments and which businesses to dispose of.

Some of the reasons for having a portfolio of businesses within a company are the following:

- *Risk management* Some companies that are in highly cyclical businesses invest in other industries that are less cyclical in order to reduce drastic changes in their cash generation capability.

- *Capturing market opportunities* Especially in emerging markets where local knowledge is a critical success factor, companies tend to invest in numerous unrelated industries just because when they identify an unsatisfied demand, the skill most crucial in success is local market knowledge rather than industry experience.

- *Capitalizing on key competencies* When a key competency developed within a firm gives them a competitive advantage for entering another business, it will tend to enter that business. An example is Honda's engine development competencies, which led them into numerous other industries.

- *Scope economies* An example would be Citibank's entry into the insurance business.

- *Asset specificity* When the fungibility of an asset is low, in order to limit the risks of dealing with a third party, companies are inclined to invest in a new business. An example is a steel company managing its own port facilities.

- *Inefficiencies in capital markets* When equity or debt markets do not function efficiently, a company that is successful in one industry and has a high cash generation capacity serves as a bank or an investor in new fields. This is more common in emerging markets.

As conditions change, companies make changes in their business portfolios. Such mergers and acquisitions activity creates more value when the assets are employed by those who can create the best value, whether because of economies of scale, economies of scope, or other synergies.

For example, many pharmaceutical companies tend to build their new product pipelines, not only by using their own R&D departments but also by acquiring startups by scientists. This is so because, while new product development may require the high level of intellectual commitment which is more likely in startups, success in the marketplace requires a good distribution capability which is available in large pharmaceutical companies. A similar approach has been followed by Cisco in another high-tech industry, namely telecoms.

In industries where economies of scale are important, consolidation is a value-creating activity. Economies of scale may be present not only in production facilities but also, and increasingly, in R&D activity, marketing, and access to distribution channels.

Another reason for portfolio restructuring is changing or increasing the strategic focus of a company. Companies that decide to grow in new fields tend to dispose of other businesses. A case in point is Nokia selling its cable business to focus on cellular business.

Those who fail to identify and act upon such portfolio restructuring opportunities on a timely basis find themselves at competitively disadvantaged positions. Hence one of the key board responsibilities is to keep an eye open for corporate transactions and closely follow others' actions.

Corporate transactions are significant investments that involve high risks. Therefore, being mentally prepared for them well in advance of a potential transaction is important. Hence, a board needs to watch the valuations and firing power (cash generation and debt or equity raising capability) of its company, as well as those of potential competitors. Therefore, relations with current and potential investors and creditors are a key area for a board's focus.

Another aspect of portfolio strategy is to identify which new businesses to develop or enter. In doing so, companies need to identify the key drivers of the new business and to determine why they would be the best placed to have the right competencies for this business. While this is the key to identifying value creation opportunities, it is also critical to analyzing how to capture a fair share of the value created. In industries where required competencies are not unique and are widely available, the ability to create entry barriers and capture value would be minimal.

In new business development projects, companies start generally with pilot projects to test the market. While this methodology aims to limit initial risks, it entails risks of its own as well. For example, small experiments may not provide the benefits of economies of scale. Also, unless scaling-up plans are prepared well in advance, adequate resource planning and capturing the market may be difficult to achieve even if the pilot is successful.

In stable industries where market information and relationships are important, incumbents may be at an advantage. However, devising strategies which are difficult for the incumbents to follow may bring a competitive advantage. For example, when Dell entered the PC market using direct sales, it was difficult for the incumbents that had established dealership networks to follow suit.

In short, a well-thought-out strategy is the key to success in entering a new business.

CHOOSING AND COACHING TOP MANAGEMENT

The most important asset of an organization is its human resources. Sustainable success requires an ability to attract, develop, and retain the right people for the organization.

Therefore, a key responsibility of the board is to ensure that the organization has the right leadership, personnel, human resources systems, and policies.

One of the key risk areas in developing new products, new markets, or new channels is the lack of people with the right skills sets and experience. Generally, evaluations of the feasibility studies for such studies focus on the financial aspects. However, if the human resources aspect of new projects is not considered properly, the likelihood of failure is high. Also, in order to be able to capture each opportunity as it arises, such as an acquisition, it is important to be able to deploy enough qualified people who have internalized the corporate culture in order to have a smooth post-merger integration. Therefore, human resources planning should be done with an eye toward future needs, and not just current ones.

As the boards are responsible for preparing the company for the future they have to consider the following questions in order to be able to evaluate the top management's approach to human resources:

- Have you identified the competencies required to implement the strategy? Do you have enough people with these competencies? If the answers are not yet affirmative, what is your hiring and development plan?

- Do you have a system for identifying, evaluating, and developing high-potential individuals? Is it functioning well? Is there a committee that oversees this process and the development of the high-potential candidates?

- Are we providing a diversity of experience to employees so as to prepare them for future responsibilities? Is people development a key performance area for managers? If you don't measure, you cannot improve. Therefore, apart from business results, another key component of manager performance should be people development.

- Do our people, as well as potential hires, believe that our company provides great development opportunities? Do we have independent measurements of such sentiments? Are employee satisfaction surveys and studies regarding corporate reputation shared with the board?

A key determinant of growth is the quality of the human resources of a company. In order to attract, develop, and retain qualified people successful companies evaluate their personnel not only on their current performance, but also on their possession of the willingness and self-discipline to develop themselves. For example, if an individual is likely to assume a new leadership position in the near future, providing coaching and helping his mental preparation for the new challenges increase his potential for success.

Organizational Structures

In order to be able to implement strategy, an appropriate organizational structure has to be designed, and the leadership of the organization determined and motivated. This is as important as the strategy itself, because a strategy not properly implemented cannot create value. The structure, processes, competencies, culture, and reward mechanisms of the organization have to be aligned with the strategy.

Therefore, organizational structure is not an end in itself, but a means to implement the strategy. As the context, the conditions, or the strategy change the structure has to be adapted to these changes as well.

One common organizational mistake is lethargy toward change – sticking to legacy systems. Many organizations reflect the realities of the past or the balance of powers established at an earlier stage, rather than the requirements of the current strategy.

Steps in any organizational study must include the following:

First, clarify and achieve consensus on the strategy and strategic goals.

Second, take into account the skills and competencies of the people within the organization, since it is difficult to change them all. Without such an assessment, the effectiveness of the organization's strategy implementation may suffer.

Third, build the organization around the key business processes in which the organization has to perform well in order to reach its strategic goals. This will increase the effectiveness. The financial, technological, and information infrastructures of the company also influence the organization design.

Fourth, determine which activities to carry out inside the organization and which ones to outsource. A lean organization is easier to manage. It is therefore important to ensure that each position and level is designed to create value.

Fifth, clearly assign authority and responsibilities to each position, and identify key performance indicators (KPIs) and determine SMART (Specific, Measurable, Actionable, Reasonable, Time-bound) goals for those KPIs.

Another issue is deciding the title for each position. Avoiding title inflation, and at the same time preserving the credibility of employees in their relationships with other stakeholders, are important considerations in assigning titles.

Sixth, determine how to handle and promote expertise development in various job families. The general tendency is to promote technically successful people to management levels, regardless of the basis of their success. Unfortunately, too often this may result in assigning a great technical person to a small management job where he may not be able to perform well, thereby losing a great technical person and getting an unsuccessful manager. Thus, an organizational structure that appropriately rewards skills development and technical excellence is an important organizational goal.

Seventh and finally, establish properly functioning information flow, reporting, and performance-rewarding systems.

Organization is the sum of all decisions on each of these dimensions and to the extent that each decision is consistent with the strategy, the likelihood of success increases.

Management Styles

Organizations are living organisms and, despite the best of designs, unless led well may not produce the desired results. Therefore, one of the key decisions is who is to lead the organization. Choice of the CEO is one of the most important decisions a board takes. The choice may change, depending on the positioning of the company. The key is the consistency of the leadership style with the strategy of the company.

For example, the leadership style required in a military organization would differ significantly from the leadership style likely to succeed in a design center. Similarly, the leadership skills required at startup may differ from those needed at maturity. Thus, identifying the dimensions of leadership styles and the choices in each dimension can well be useful in identifying the right leader at the right time for the organization.

Strategic Direction

The first dimension of leadership style is how to decide on the **strategic direction**. There are three different styles within this dimension:

- *Visionary leadership* This style is utilized by leaders who motivate the organization around a vision which is innovative and exciting for the organization. Steve Jobs is a good example.

- *Top-down leadership* This is utilized by authoritative leaders and is applicable when significant resources are needed to implement key decisions, and the leader is involved in planning and implementing the details of the decisions.

- *Participative leadership* This style is utilized by social leaders. Organizations that need numerous decisions to respond to market and customer trends tend to prefer distributed decision-making. Open communication, experimentation, and empowerment are critical for success in this type of leadership.

Corporate Values and Culture

The second dimension of leadership is **corporate values and culture**. Four different approaches are identified within this dimension:

- *Entrepreneurship and innovation* Under this culture, initiative-taking and creativity are promoted. 3M is a good example.

- *Teamwork* Transparency, mutual trust, and joint work are promoted.

- *Internal competition* Here there is a high-stress environment where individual performance is the key to success and there is strong competition between employees for better performance. Many investment banks fall into this category.

- *Operational excellence and discipline* Consistent attention to detail and continuous improvement are promoted under this culture. Toyota may be a good example.

Accountability and Controls

The third dimension of leadership relates to **accountability** and **controls**. There are three different approaches:

- *Human focus* Professional and ethical standards and values are the primary tools for establishing the corporate culture. This approach is preferred especially when it is difficult to measure the relationship between inputs and outputs, as in creative jobs, for example.

- *Financial results focus* When multiple decisions, each of which involves limited resource allocations, such as establishing customer contact points, are critical for the success of the corporation, results provide the best control mechanism.

- *Operational excellence focus* For companies involved in mass production where continuous process improvement is important for business success, this approach is preferred. Key performance indicators, and responsibility and authority charts, have to be developed to monitor developments closely.

How to Develop Competencies

The fourth dimension of management style is how to develop competencies. Four different approaches can be observed:

- *Process-oriented development of intellectual capital* Systems are more important than individual competencies. For example, establishing a CRM system takes precedence over developing individual sales competencies; rotations and multiple interfaces with customers' decision-makers are common.

- *Promoting from within* Employee loyalty is promoted. On-the-job training and employee development programs receive primary focus. Annual performance reviews place particular emphasis on skills development initiatives.

- *Hiring the best* The key feature is keeping an eye open for the best performers in the industry and giving attractive packages so as to be the employer of choice. This approach is seen most widely in fast-growing companies, where it is difficult to match the speed of people development with the growth of the company.

- *Outsourcing or business partnerships* This approach is applied not only for non-core activities, but also for core activities where managing a network of highly capable individuals is preferred to hiring them. It is preferred especially in highly creative industries. One example would be utilizing a network of designers.

Relationship Management

The fifth dimension of management style is relationship management.

- *Employee focus* When the most important relationship is with customers and distribution channels, customer representatives tend to be key employees, whereas when productivity is the key then systems engineers and quality people tend to be more important.

- *Competition focus* The key to success is to follow the moves of competitors very closely and devise tactics to counter them.

- *Business partner relationships* Distributors of international brands or local joint venture partners of global firms tend to fall especially into this category, because the most important relationship to manage is this one.

- *Regulatory agency relationships* Particularly in industries such as energy, and telecommunications, the key relationship to manage is the regulatory agency relationship.

Therefore, in evaluating and choosing the most appropriate management style, making an assessment in each of these dimensions will be useful for the board.

Choosing the CEO

A captain's competence cannot be tested in calm seas.

Lukianos

In order to be able to make an appropriate choice of CEO, the board has to have a deep understanding of the company, the environment, and potential candidates. Many boards establish a nomination committee to better evaluate the potential candidates, in terms not only of their achievements but also of their values and their management styles. Members of such a committee need to pay special attention to independence, confidentiality, fairness, and the exercising of sound judgment. Generally, one of the members is a former CEO of the company so as to be able to provide special insights into the requirements of the job. However, special attention should also be paid to ensuring that the committee is not dominated by such an individual and that a fair discussion of the pros and cons of each candidate, internal or external, takes place.

A sensitive issue is differentiation between a good manager and a good leader. A successful manager, who **does the job right** (manages a function or task well), need not be a good a leader, who **does the right job** (takes the initiative in deciding what to do.) But generally, as the CEO is responsible for implementation, he should be both a good manager and a good leader.

A successful CEO needs to have a number of characteristics. First and foremost is the ability to **set a vision** for the company and to **focus every resource** on realizing this vision. The ability to deal with complexity and to focus corporate resources on a common vision improves the effectiveness of resource utilization.

Another key characteristic of a good CEO is **high ethical standards**. The tone at the top determines the tune in the middle. As one of the key responsibilities of the CEO is not only to create value but also to preserve the value of the resources they control, their performance is predicated not only upon short-term results but also upon the sustainability of the corporation. Any departure from high ethical standards seriously harms the sustainability of the organization. Furthermore, a CEO with high ethical standards improves the trustworthiness of the corporation and becomes a role model for the rest of the organization.

A good CEO needs to have good communication skills and an ability to motivate people around them. In today's organizations, spanning a number of geographies, the ability to keep people throughout the organization motivated and focused on the vision requires good communication and persuasion skills. Any organization that is to be successful needs to mobilize not only its own resources but also the resources of all its stakeholders. Therefore, the CEO has to spend significant amounts of time with shareholders, creditors, potential investors, management teams, employees, suppliers, regulators, communities, and all other stakeholders. The CEO's performance has a significant impact on mobilizing resources for the vision of the company.

Good management requires teamwork. Therefore, one of the key characteristics of a good CEO is their ability to select, develop, and motivate people. Having a good understanding of the strengths and weaknesses of each team member and how to motivate them is an important leadership skill. Good leadership is also being a good coach. Therefore, what is important is not only forming a good team, but also developing the people in it. The more important aspects of leadership may be summarized as follows:

Leadership

Leadership is the ability to activate people towards a common goal. On average, each person changes the actions of 250 people in one form or another. In this sense, everyone is a leader. However, what makes great leaders is; the number of people influenced, the impact and sustainability of the change, and the size of resources mobilized for the common goal.

A leader has the ability to motivate all employees towards a common vision and provides the confidence to overcome any difficulties that may be faced on the way to the vision.

Leadership development necessitates watching not only the performance of the people in their current position, but also competencies they have that could be utilized in other positions. Ability to take initiatives, motivate others, demonstrate discipline to deliver results, ability to influence outside networks, communication and people development skills are particularly evaluated.

Good management skills such as making challenging but realistic budgets and delivering them, developing others, using resources effectively, and establishing and monitoring internal controls, as well as demonstrating high ethical standards, are also closely watched in order to identify future leaders.

A CEO needs to be decisive. They have to be able to make tough decisions under conditions of uncertainty. In many instances being indecisive or a populist will hurt the company. Therefore, a good CEO needs to have a high degree of self-confidence to face reality and take decisions with less than perfect knowledge. Having a high degree of self-confidence does not mean omnipotence, but accepting the fact that taking no decision is the worst decision.

While not being indecisive even under uncertainty, CEOs need to be open to conflicting information. Adapting to changing conditions does not mean indecisiveness. A good captain has to be able to judge the weather conditions and alter course if necessary in order to reach the destination.

Also, the ability to take precautions and manage risks is a key leadership skill. Preparing the minds of the leadership team for potential risks helps to identify early signs in different risk areas and to deal with them effectively.

In short, a good CEO, with their values, decisions, communication, and behavior, is a role model.

Therefore, in choosing a CEO the board members need to feel comfortable that they know the candidates well in order to be able to evaluate them from each of these perspectives.

Another issue for the board to watch is not only the choice of the CEO, but also the ability of the organization to develop future leaders. The depth of the bench is a critical issue for the sustainability of the corporation. GE is a good example of a company that takes this issue seriously. While many Fortune 500 firms suffer during CEO transitions, GE consistently develops people and establishes a competitive selection process. Even the losers in this process can turn out to be great CEOs elsewhere.

In choosing leaders, we need to focus on competencies required to deliver the strategy for the corporation, not on characteristics like "familiar", "attractive," or "one of our own." Some common mistakes made in the selection of leaders are:

Common Leadership Selection Pitfalls

- Public speaking skills are taken as an important indicator of communication skills. While public speaking is an important leadership skill, so is the ability to persuade others in small meetings. As this is more difficult to observe, less weight is given to this skill. However, this is a critical skill for a CEO.

- Also, many physical characteristics such as height and beauty that are irrelevant for leadership seem often to influence the choice of leaders.

- Being a conforming team member is considered to be a positive characteristic. However, feeling uncomfortable about being a dissident voice may be a weakness in leadership. Someone too prone to conformity may build a team that would not challenge the leadership, and this may lead to groupthink.

- Problem-solving skills are also considered to be important. However, leadership requires a future orientation, an ability to take the initiative and benefit from opportunities, rather than focusing solely on problem-solving. Therefore, strategic thinking skills are more important than problem-solving skills.

- The performance of each candidate is scrutinized, but not necessarily the performance of the members of the candidate's team, which is a better indicator of the candidate's people development skills.

One of the key indicators of a successful organization is its ability to develop and export leaders.

Performance Management and Reward Systems

The ability to attract, retain, and motivate a competent leadership team is a critical ingredient in successful performance. Therefore, compensation and performance management systems are of critical importance.

Unless the business processes are well defined and key performance indicators are properly established, it is not possible to measure performance. There are certain principles to follow for a good compensation and performance management system.

The goal of the compensation and performance management system is to attract, retain, develop, and motivate a competent leadership team and focus them on sustainable value creation. Given the intricacies of the issue, most boards establish a separate compensation committee to address compensation systems and parameters. It is recommended that this committee be made up of independent members. The committee has to establish its own agenda, monitor developments in the market for managers, have the ability to receive independent advice, and preferably hold separate meetings to establish the parameters of the compensation system and to make evaluations of the performance of the management.

The compensation committee has to be able to hire independent advisors. Preferably these advisors should not have any other business with the company; at the least, any other work must be pre-approved by the board and the total amount of their work reported in the company's annual report to the annual shareholders' meeting.

The key issues that need to be handled in the compensation and performance system are the following:

- Determining the key performance indicators for the company.

- Testing the parameters of the compensation and reward system under different scenarios and under past performance realizations.

- Predetermining what will be considered as attractive rewards for extraordinary performance, and normal (not excessive) rewards for normal performance.

- Making sure that performance is evaluated on a comparative basis with competitors. Benchmarking performance against competitors is one of the best ways to normalize performance for industry and economic conditions.

For publicly traded companies especially it is recommended that the management rewards are aligned with the returns enjoyed by shareholders. Any share ownership by management should have certain restrictions, in particular strict guidelines for insider trading and blackout periods. Such policies should be made available publicly. Also in line with the transparency principle, the compensation of top management should be fully reported in the company's annual reports, alongside the relevant comparative data for competitors. The compensation disclosures should include not only current compensation but also estimates of earned future benefits as well.

In short, top management compensation is a key governance issue that needs to be handled with due care and transparency.

QUALITY OF COMMUNICATION

The effectiveness of a board is linked directly to the quality of the communication between the board members, between the board and the management, and between the board and the other stakeholders. This is so because the main board responsibilities of providing guidance and oversight influence others' behaviors. Influence can be exerted properly only if the decisions are communicated clearly and persuasively.

No one is as wise as all of us. Therefore, board members who are responsible for approving such critical issues as strategy, top management appointments, and risk appetite for their companies make collective decisions. Hence the sincerity, accuracy, and authenticity of the communication within the board improve the quality of collective decision-making. Transparent, open communication and trust among the board members are key to being able to consider and address every aspect of each board decision in a balanced way.

The most important sins to avoid are lack of sincerity and keeping information away from the board members. The best measure of good communication between board members and between the board and management is to have **no surprises**. Any behavior that would create such a feeling would not only undermine adequate consideration of the issue at hand, but also poison the climate of healthy communication.

Another issue to consider is the separation of data from opinions. It is therefore important to provide the board with current data that are benchmarked with past performances, budgets, and other competitors. An assurance process for how data is gathered is also important for the credibility of the results derived from the data.

When opinions are being expressed, it is healthier to keep them impersonal. Therefore, the role of chairperson is a critical one in creating the right climate to ensure that every aspect of the issue at hand is considered properly before reaching a conclusion.

It is also important to conduct the communication in a constructive tone, even when it involves criticism of management proposals. The role of the board is not to find fault but to increase the quality of the decisions. Good communication skills include good listening skills.

A board is a collective decision-making body. Therefore, rather than having each member communicate their own views to the stakeholders, it is imperative to have a unified voice; this is communicated by the chairperson or the lead director, or else the responsibility may be delegated to the management. The chairperson may have a role in communicating with the shareholders and investors; however, the communication with other stakeholders is generally handled by the CEO.

Key to sustainable success is strict adherence to corporate values and culture. Therefore, the board should consider not only performance results but also how they are achieved. Hence, the board's communications should not only involve its decisions but should also pay particular attention to strict adherence to stated corporate values so as to ensure that the tone at the top is translated accurately throughout the organization.

In short, the effectiveness of a board depends on open, sincere, accurate, authentic, and constructive communication that creates a climate where each board-level issue is properly considered in terms of the potential impacts on various stakeholders.

Investor Relations

Key stakeholders for publicly traded companies are the current and potential shareholders. Timely and open communication with the investors is the basis for establishing credibility within the financial markets. One of the key responsibilities of a board is to ensure that the company has a credible investor relations strategy and implementation. Timely and accurate disclosure that goes beyond statutory requirements and compliance matters is the key to gaining the trust of the investor community. In short, **a successful investor relations program means no surprises.**

The counterparties for investor relations consist of a wide range of individuals and institutions such as: shareholders, potential investors (individual and institutional), analysts, brokerage houses, investment banks, debt holders, rating agencies, and financial media. Therefore, the investor relations program should cover concurrent communication with all counterparties.

The primary goal of investor relations is to expand the group of investors and analysts following the company, to gain their trust, and to position the company for an effective future secondary listing, bond issuance, or loan syndication when and if such a need arises, and to do this in a cost-effective manner. This can be achieved only if information is shared in a way that is clear, timely, and transparent.

A key principle of investor relations is to provide the same information to all shareholders concurrently. Many companies are utilizing webcasts and their company websites to enable all who are interested to follow the shareholder general meetings and analysts' meetings or presentations to avoid unfair treatment.

Another key principle of investor relations is the timely disclosure of triggering events. Therefore, establishing a clear process and clear responsibilities for identifying and disclosing triggering events and monitoring performance is a key board responsibility. The company should also regularly disclose key governance issues such as:

- The process for identifying and choosing board and committee members, with special emphasis on their independence.

- Qualifications of board members and top management, as well as their compensation.

- Board and committee charters, ethical standards, related party transactions, and insider-trading activity during non-blackout periods.

Corporate events that will trigger a disclosure may be summarized as follows:

Triggering Events for Disclosure

- Entry into or termination of material definitive agreements, involving significant corporate transactions such as M&As and the sale or purchase of assets that would have a significant impact on the balance sheet.

- Completion of corporate transactions or asset sales/purchases.

- Any material issue that would change the quarterly financials in a material way.

- Creation of a material financial obligation on- or off-balance-sheet, such as guarantees.

- Any event instigating a direct or indirect financial obligation.

- Costs associated with exit or disposal activities.

- Material impairments of the value of corporate assets.

- Bankruptcy or failure to adhere to key financial covenants.

- Any board decision that may impact the rights of shareholders.

- Changes in control.

- Changes in board memberships or top management.

- Amendments to articles of incorporation or by-laws.

The tools for investor relations include annual reports, the disclosure of quarterly financial results, disclosures of special events, websites, presentations to analysts and the financial press, road shows and shareholders' general meetings. While the CEO and CFO generally lead the investor relations programs, it is advisable to provide access to the chairperson or lead director in order for the board to have the ability to address any investor concerns that may arise.

Investor relations is a two-way street. Receiving the concerns or views of the investment community is just as important as the information provided to them. Receiving feedback from the investor community on issues they have identified or their likely reactions to key corporate moves provides a valuable input to management decisions. Also, relations with investors may be a valuable source of information about potential mergers and acquisition activity in the industry. A board needs to monitor market perceptions about the company, market consensus about its performance, and market reactions to key management initiatives.

Evaluation of the investor relations function requires information about the investor relations strategy, the calendar of activities, and staff development. Tools such as investor perception surveys, road show feedback, analyst reports, articles in the financial media, and direct communication with key investors provide inputs to effective investor relations.

The board, and in particular the corporate governance committee, should regularly receive information about the following:

1. Share performance, including price, volume, trends, and benchmarks with peers.

2. Analysts' consensus estimates and comparisons with plans and projections, and peer group comparisons.

3. Market perceptions about the company strategy and share valuations.

4. Other issues raised by investors and analysts.

5. Share ownership patterns: who owns how much and how the shareholder profile changes.

6. The strategy and implementation program of the investor relations function, including the review of the annual report, company website, and company presentations, as well as benchmarking of the investor relations department's activities with the best-in-class examples.

As a key element of investor communications, the annual reports have to be simple, clear, comprehensive, consistent, and concise:

- **Simplicity** refers to the ability of a non-expert to be able to understand.

- **Clarity** refers to the ease of finding relevant information within the report and the availability of benchmarks to establish relevance.

- **Comprehensiveness** refers to the coverage of all the relevant issues and risks, and being understandable without reference to other reports.

- **Consistency** refers to the ability to follow issues and developments over time.

- **Being concise** refers to being precise and to the point.

The content of the information to be shared with the investor community should include the mission and vision of the company, the evaluation of the industry and business environment, key strategies and indicators as to how to follow the developments in the strategic direction, financial performance indicators, investor presentations, disclosures about key developments, key shareholders and creditors, important developments in the value chain and in particular information about the key suppliers and customers, corporate social responsibility initiatives, and corporate governance issues.

It is important to make sure that data on these dimensions are provided in a comparative format with the past performance and other benchmarks, are verifiable by independent third parties, and are comprehensive enough to cover all relevant issues and risk areas.

Companies that implement a successful investor relations program are more likely to gain both the trust of the investor community and visibility. This in turn helps the company when it needs to raise capital or borrowing for major projects or inorganic growth opportunities. It also helps to access diverse pools of investment, to increase in corporate reputation, and to gain speed and cost effectiveness in raising additional capital when needed.

In short, winning the trust of the investor community helps in winning against the competition. Oversight of the investor relations strategy and processes, as well as ensuring that accurate information is shared with the community on a timely basis, is a board responsibility.

"RIGHT GUIDANCE" – SUMMARY

One of the most important responsibilities of a board is to provide strategic guidance to the corporation. However in doing so, its decisions, behaviors, and communications also shape the corporate culture. Therefore, walking the talk and openly following the corporate governance principles is critical to making sure that the tone at the top gets translated into the tune in the organization.

Consistency   Consistency is a key test of successful strategy. Also, the alignment of incentives for management and the successful implementation of the corporate strategy are key board responsibilities.

Responsibility   The essence of strategy is choice. Making a choice inevitably involves risk-taking. Understanding the key risks of the strategic choice, ensuring that those risks are adequately managed, and monitoring progress are key board responsibilities.

Accountability   The board is responsible for the setting the standards of accountability and management style of the CEO, through the choice it makes of the top management as well as by demanding a culture of transparency and the effectiveness of internal controls.

Fairness   Motivation of the management can be attained only if the board is seen to be fair in making performance evaluations and in management compensation.

Transparency   Transparency in challenging strategic alternatives and aligning management incentives with the strategy helps improve the quality of implementation.

Effectiveness   Focusing on the right issues and considering every aspect of strategic alternatives increases the effectiveness of the guidance provided by the board.

Deployment   A key benefit of the strategy development process is the mental preparation of the organization. Hence deployment of strategic guidance throughout the organization improves the responsiveness of the company to strategic threats and opportunities.

CHAPTER 7

Right Oversight

All power tends to corrupt; absolute power corrupts absolutely.

Lord Acton

INTERNAL CONTROLS

One of the key responsibilities of the board of directors is **to ensure** that there are **effective oversight** and **internal controls** for the company. Therefore, internal and external auditors that provide assurance for the effectiveness of internal control systems are responsible to the board. The main purpose of internal controls is to create a culture of disciplined behavior by identifying any real or potential lapses by individuals from corporate policies.

However, the tendency of the audit function to move toward a mechanistic, rule-based process that judges management decisions on a retrospective basis, should be avoided. Establishing a culture of accountability and transparency should be the key goal.

The board of directors has the joint role of establishing the rules and judging the management. Therefore, the conduct of the directors and their communications with the management is critical to preventing the evolution of a normative and formalist corporate culture that would estrange the management and limit shareholder value growth. The board should be especially careful not to undermine the management and not to have any tendency to micromanage the company from the boardroom. Otherwise, initiative-taking within the company will be seriously hampered and all decisions, whether strategic or not, will be brought to the board, effectively slowing the company down.

The board should never lose sight of the fact that **their most important role is to improve shareholder value**, and increasing shareholder value involves appropriate risk-taking. Therefore, has to have an allowance to "push the envelope" with sufficient zeal any management that does its job properly.

An important risk that the auditing function should be careful about is to avoid the transformation of the management system from a results-oriented system to a control-oriented mechanism. In the public sector especially, each time a problem is unearthed a new rule is established to prevent such a situation, leading to a bureaucratization of the sector which limits the initiative-taking propensity of the public-sector managers.

In order to be able to establish a sound audit process, the **authority levels** and **approval mechanisms** for decision-making have to be clearly established. If there are too many issues to be decided and approved by the board then the decision-making processes will slow down and the learning mechanisms will be weakened. For this reason, **only key strategic decisions** should require approval by the board of directors.

In order for decisions to be subject to auditing, a **record** of the decisions **should be kept** and assessed by an independent unit. For this reason, the determination of how each decision will be recorded is an important requirement. In addition, decision-makers at all levels should be able to explain the reasons for their decisions in line with the principles of **accountability** and **transparency**.

In order to ensure that decision-making is done in an effective manner, the record-keeping and explanation process should be operated efficiently. There should be no reluctance at board level to question the management on their decisions for fear of giving offense. By the same token, an overly skeptical, critical attitude by the board may not only be too time-consuming for the management, but also create a sense of constant mistrust which could be detrimental to the company. The balance between creating a culture of initiative-taking and a culture of accountability and transparency about the reasons for decisions is vital if oversight is to be effective.

A satisfactory oversight process should consider not only the results but also **the decision-making process**. In order to ensure continuous improvement, the evaluation process should determine whether there is an internal review procedure where the explicit or implicit assumptions for the decisions are systematically reviewed, and policy changes, when necessary, are implemented.

In many institutions, the audit function focuses on the discipline maintained in applying the internal procedures. However, while this is important, if the sole focus of the audit process is procedural, it may result in bureaucratization and losing sight of the business results.

For a public company especially, the timely provision of accurate information is a key regulatory and market requirement. While the primary responsibility rests with the management, it is also the responsibility of the audit committee and the board to establish an effective internal process to ensure that each disclosure requirement is met on a timely and comprehensive basis.

Generally, any company above a particular size and area of operation establishes an internal audit department. The decision to institute an internal auditing function should be taken by the audit committee of the board, the CEO, and the chief financial officer (CFO).

In some companies the internal auditing function works under the CFO, in others under the CEO, and in some directly under the auditing committee of the management board. More recent trends are toward establishing a direct link between the internal auditing function and the auditing committee of the board. This is with the aim especially of ensuring independence of the internal audit function in:

- Investigations of fraud.

- The identification of violations of codes of conduct or ethical codes.

- Being able to bring to the board's attention any occasion where the top management's actions are perceived not to be sufficiently sensitive in high-risk areas.

However, this organizational independence to ensure objectivity should not be taken as having a special status within the company. The employees of the internal auditing department should not be subject to a different personnel regime. The internal auditing department is linked operationally to the management. **Internal audit** is an **important support function** for departments such as human resources, planning and budgeting, and information technology. For this reason, no matter which level internal auditing is linked to within the internal corporate hierarchy, the weight of the positions should be evaluated in the same manner as the other support functions. The size of this department, just like any other support department, should be determined using cost–benefit analysis.

One attitude that is essential to avoid in internal auditing is acting like a prosecutor and evaluating the management decisions solely on their results on a retrospective basis. Management is the art of decision-making and taking risks with less than full information. Again, therefore, it would be unrealistic to expect a 100% batting average from management. Such an expectation would not only hinder initiative-taking, but would also encourage slow decision-making, which as a result will harm the success of the company.

Establishing the control mechanisms, and **making them operational** in the company, **is primarily a management responsibility**, not an audit responsibility. For this reason, the responsibility of the internal auditing department of working with and supporting the management should be carefully considered. This perception can prevail only if it is supported by the members of the audit committee, the executive management, and the chief of internal audit unit.

Internal auditing, except where the executive management is suspected of involvement in fraud, should be conducted not against the management but in a supportive and value-creating manner. **The internal audit function should have the goal of bringing a systematic, disciplined approach to evaluating and improving the effectiveness of risk management, internal controls, and governance processes.**

Internal audit is composed of three different types of auditing:

- Financial auditing.
- Compliance auditing.
- Operational auditing.

Financial auditing is conducted to keep the corporate records accurate and up-to-date. In addition, it is done to guarantee that the financial and management reporting is based on corporate records that are reliable and verifiable. The assessment of the practices and risks involved in the protection of the value of company assets are included in this framework. In general, the materiality limit determined for internal audit is lower than the limit for external audit. For this reason, internal audit needs more continuous and detailed work, which helps the regular assessment of the effectiveness of corporate control systems. Here is the current definition of materiality, with some of the common rules pertaining to it listed below:

Materiality

Materiality is defined by the International Accounting Standards Board (IASB) as follows:

Information is material if its omission or misstatement could influence the economic decision of users taken on the basis of the financial statements. Materiality depends on the size of the item or error judged in the particular circumstances of its omission or misstatement. Thus, materiality provides a threshold or cut-off point rather than being a primary qualitative characteristic which information must have if it is to be useful.

Some common rules that have appeared in practice and academia to quantify materiality include:

- Percentage of pre-tax income or net income.
- Percentage of gross profit.
- Percentage of total assets.
- Percentage of total revenue.
- Percentage of equity.
- Blended methods involving some or all of these definitions.
- "Sliding-scale" methods which vary with the size of the entity.

Audit committees are often responsible for setting the threshold for "planning materiality," which affects the scope of both tests of controls and substantive tests as well as the costs of auditing.

Compliance auditing is done to determine whether the activities of the company are in line with laws, decrees, company policies and procedures, and the ethical code of the company.

Operational auditing is future-oriented and assesses whether the company activities are suitable to achieve the company mission, vision, and strategies. Also, operational auditing is used to assure that the company undertakes activities effectively and efficiently.

The unit that conducts **the internal audit function** should grasp that risk management is a management function. The unit should perceive that **its role is to support the management** by questioning and developing proposals. Similarly, the executive management should view the internal audit function as an important support service. The management should invite the chief of the auditing unit to management meetings so that the unit is kept up-to-date about **the issues that are currently important for the company.**

The internal audit department ensures that the processes and systems for the identification and assessment of the risks facing the company are adequately questioned and continuously improved. The department provides reviews to ensure that risk management systems are used regularly, and works to determine that information about the risks and precautions against important risks are assessed within the governance system. However, **decisions about the risks to be** taken, the precautions to lower the risks, or decisions to be taken about insurance are a responsibility not of the internal audit but of management.

The major role of the internal audit is to present an objective, independent assessment and to support the use of a systematic, disciplined, and reliable approach in the risk management of the company. In advanced applications, an internal control function may be conducted by management using **self-assessment** methods. Here, the internal audit function would perform statistical control procedures to see if the self-assessment processes are conducted appropriately, use a disciplined approach, and contain best practices.

New technologies provide opportunities to institute "**continuous monitoring systems.**" Systems such as SAP provide for many business processes to be conducted and recorded electronically, thereby allowing authority levels to be defined in the system. Hence decisions and processes can be monitored on a real-time basis. When such continuous monitoring systems are established within a company, the resources of the internal audit departments can be focused on higher-risk areas and system improvement functions.

In addition, internal auditing can provide consultancy to management on:

- Ethical codes.

- The potential conflict of interests.

- The establishment of control mechanisms when important projects are initiated and/or when information systems are renewed.

In short, internal auditing is an important function to ensure that management and control processes work well within the organization. Development of this function requires that the focus is on the essence of risk management, control, and governance processes, not on rules-based procedures, and that the initiative-taking ability of the management is not hindered.

RISK MANAGEMENT

Risk management is the essence of management In order to maintain the sustainability of corporate governance and achieve business success, risk management should be conducted systematically. For this reason, it is important that risk management is reflected in the attitude of managers toward the business and translated into every business process. The role of the board of directors is to ensure that the processes established by management in this area are sound and reliable. **Prudent risk management is the key to the sustainability of organizations.**

Prudent risk management is key to successful entrepreneurship. The most successful Turkish entrepreneur, the late Vehbi Koç, with whom I had the honor to work, used to ask the question, "How much could I lose?", when trying to determine the potential value-at-risk, as the first question of any investment decision. He would not go ahead with any investment, regardless of the feasibility of the project, if the value-at-risk was too large for him to bear.

In evaluating the risks and returns of a potential investment, one of the key points to pay attention to is that the expected return has to be a function of the inherent risk profile of the industry. For example, industries such as electricity generation have longer payback periods, reflecting the relatively low risk profile of the industry.

In order to be able to manage risk the board needs the following:

- **Mental preparation** Identification of risks requires a good understanding of the industry and of competitive dynamics, as well as of social, economic, political, technological, and environmental trends. Improvement in the competencies of foresight requires not only a wide range of sources of information, but also alternative action plans prepared on the basis of scenario analysis and simulation.

- **Risk-sharing** The reasons for forming joint ventures in mega projects include not only fund-raising but also risk-sharing. Risks can be shared not only with joint venture partners, but also with suppliers or customers.

- **Diversification** One of the key reasons for having more conglomerates in emerging markets where social and economic risks are higher is risk diversification. The key to having good risk diversification is to operate in different industries which have low correlation with the business cycles of each other.

- **Financial prudence** Utilizing a lower debt/equity ratio, emphasis on cash balances, and lower currency or term mismatches in the balance sheets are tools commonly employed by the prudent in highly volatile emerging markets.

The boards would be well advised to ask the CEO to regularly update them on the following risk areas:

- Developments in financial markets

- Technological developments

- Regulatory developments

- Social trends and tensions

- Political developments in the relevant jurisdictions

- Environmental and safety issues, both for workers as well as for customers and other elements of the value chain

- Reputational risks

- Shifts in industry trends are potential new entrants to industry

Risk management is basically a function of executive management. The scope, the organization, and the operation of this function are determined by the CEO. Any suggestion that risk management is not a part of the CEO's responsibility is equivalent to undermining the management responsibility of the CEO. In order to be successful in business life, risks should be managed and the CEO should be at peace with the risks. Without any risk, there will not be any gain. **Business is the art of undertaking calculated risks for competitive advantage. Therefore, risk should not be avoided but managed.**

Risk Preparedness

Evaluating potential risks and contingencies for dealing with them should regularly be on the board agenda. This is so, because **luck favors the prepared mind.**

In the business world risks may be analyzed in three categories:

1. Financial risks.

2. Operational risks.

3. Strategic risks. Strategic risks in turn may be categorized in seven dimensions:

    (i)   Project risk.

    (ii)   Customer risk.

    (iii) Change management risk.

(iv) Competitor risk.

(v) Reputational risk.

(vi) Industry structure risk.

(vii) Economic risk.

Generally, boards will more frequently follow financial risks such as the level of customer credits or inventories. However, having a systemic review of all potential material risks and all plans for risk mitigation is good board practice.

For example, any interruption in the supply chain may pose an operational risk for the company. Therefore, companies tend to avoid working with a single supplier for critical components. Another supply chain risk may involve interruptions in pricing. For instance, currency movements or increases in transportation costs may change the economics of outsourcing from overseas markets. Similarly, a fire at a significant transportation node may lead to risks of stoppage in production facilities.

Production facilities may also be prone to failures in infrastructure systems, such as electricity supply or information systems. Health problems in critical personnel or strikes, environmental issues such as toxic material slippages, or equipment failures for lack of timely maintenance may all lead to inability to deliver. Security risks, fraud, and a deficiency in internal controls also fall into the category of internal risks.

The category of strategic risks involves competitive issues such as increases in the market power of key suppliers due to consolidation, or new market entries by new competitors with different competencies. For example, consolidation among iron ore producers influences the profitability of steel manufacturers, or the growth of supermarket chains increases their bargaining power.

Also, either major investment projects or post-merger integration issues may pose significant project risks for the company. Technological obsolescence, the deterioration of brand value, or changes in social trends are among strategic risks. For example, the move against obesity may hurt the growth prospects of fast food chains, or regulatory changes may influence the input costs of energy companies. Economic crises and fast currency movements are also among the market risks.

If risks are to be managed, then:

1. The risks have to be identified.

2. The risks have to be evaluated and prioritized.

3. Contingency plans must be prepared and regularly tested.

4. The early warning signs must be identified.

5. The early warning signs have to be monitored.

6. Mitigation investments have to be undertaken.

7. Self-insurance choices must be made.

Having a good risk management system helps companies in:

1. Establishing prudent management systems.

2. Increasing the awareness of risk-reward choices for the sake of better entrepreneurship and innovation capabilities.

3. Having consistent communication with the relevant authorities.

4. Improving stakeholder communications.

5. Acquiring greater reputational value.

6. Focusing on strategic initiatives without being derailed.

7. Long-term value creation.

Managing risk requires the development of contingency plans and the conducting of systematic dry runs. One of the reasons for the low level of casualties in the Al-Qaeda attack on HSBC's Istanbul headquarters was the level of preparedness established by having regular dry runs of the evacuation plans.

In short, while certain risks are easy to monitor from financial statements, there are many other risk categories that may have significant impacts on the company's profitability. Therefore, **a systemic identification, prioritization, and assessment of risks** and **the development of contingency plans** with the use of techniques such as scenario analysis and simulation should be a priority for the board.

The expectations of the board of directors with regard to risk management and crisis management may be summarized as follows:

1. Crisis management plans should be developed and regularly tested by the crisis management team.

2. These plans should be assessed at least once a year.

3. The plans should be checked to see whether they are consistent with the size of the company and the potential risks it faces.

4. These plans should protect the security and integrity of the corporate records; and ensure that they are accessible for business continuity purposes in case of an emergency.

5. Plans should be established for the continuity of the systems of critical importance.

6. Precautionary procedures should be set up for identifying and controlling financial and operational risks.

7. Every system that involves the company's customer, employee, supplier, regulatory, and other stakeholder data should have a backup.

8. Potential risks to other stakeholders should be assessed.

However, the perception of the management is as important as the systems, policies, and procedures in this area. Developing foresight in the areas of risk and crisis management and taking precautionary measures is not an inappropriate cost, but a requirement to ensure business continuity. To guarantee that these issues are widely acknowledged in the corporation is among the duties of the management and board of directors.

Example: IT Dependence

Developments in information technologies not only increase significantly the capacity of firms to collect, store, and use information, but also reduce the costs of doing so. Also, the effectiveness of business processes increases significantly with the ever increasing utilization of data in decision-making processes. However, while the unit cost reductions reach 30% annually, because of changes in the way business is conducted IT costs continue to increase.

While the utilization of data-based systems has significant impacts on productivity gains, competitive advantages, and internal control capabilities, increasing dependence on IT also increases risks in two major areas, namely (1) **business continuity**, and (2) **information security**. Therefore, the board needs to focus also on developments in these issues.

As the dependence of critical business processes on IT systems increases, many companies need to develop business continuity infrastructures for their IT systems. Emergency plans should be prepared and tested regularly for recovery from extended interruptions in IT services. Such an approach requires not only redundancy investments for the reliability, availability, and serviceability of alternative fault-tolerant IT sites, but also behavioral preparation of the organization for alternative scenarios. For example, an adequate business continuity plan should involve not only data duplication in an emergency center positioned at a different location, but also the identification of alternate responsibilities for those key employees who will not be able to make it to the company location owing to the lack of transportation facilities or for any other reason.

The second key issue is to protect business-critical information from unauthorized access and utilization. Here, it is vital to have a formal scheme for the authorization of access to different levels of information. And in establishing the authorization levels it is critical to observe separation of powers. No individual should have single-handed authority, and access to business-sensitive information should be restricted. The encryption of sensitive information is also good practice. Further, it is crucial to test the system regularly for its vulnerability to unauthorized access. Some companies hire ethical hackers to test their systems.

In evaluating both the business continuity risks and the information security risks, one area commonly missed is outsourced parts of the value chain. System tests and emergency simulations should involve the operation and risks of the whole value chain. Also, every company has to pay attention to improving and diversifying the competencies of mission-critical personnel, who include not only IT staff but also management and the internal control department. A systematic approach in testing, updating, and protecting IT systems is as important as it is in making the initial investment in world-class systems.

Chief Legal Officer

Another area of risk for the corporation is failure to comply with ever changing laws and regulations, and other legal issues. Therefore, many companies establish a position of chief legal officer (CLO) to identify, control, and manage such legal risks. The occupant of this position is expected not only to follow and interpret developments in the regulatory environment, but also to help the management to utilize them for competitive advantage. To fill this position they have to have not only a legal background but also a sound understanding of business issues.

In public companies especially, the CLO is expected to serve as a consultant to the management with respect to capital markets' regulation. Areas of involvement here include identifying triggering events for disclosures, declarations of blackout periods for insider trading, and drafting codes of conduct.

Another area of responsibility for the chief legal officer is participating in identification and mitigation of legal and reputational risks. Developments in corporate governance regulations such as Sarbanes-Oxley and Basel II are also reviewed, and implications for the company are identified and communicated by the legal officer. The chief legal officer also helps to provide oversight of the relations with employees and other stakeholders. In particular, adherence of suppliers to the same ethical and social standards is becoming a corporate responsibility.

Having a chief legal officer is also useful in setting the corporate standards for legal agreements and in consolidating and controlling off-balance-sheet liabilities assumed by such agreements. The legal officer also participates in establishing company policies toward voluntary corporate social responsibility standards such as the UN Global Compact. The CLO brings potential risk areas to the attention of the CEO and when necessary the board. The chief legal officer is therefore an important member of the top management team.

Audit Committee

The primary function of the audit committee is to assist the board in fulfilling its oversight responsibilities in assuring the following:

1. The quality, integrity, and appropriateness of financial statements.

2. The quality, integrity, and performance of internal controls regarding accounting, finance, operations, IT, and risk management systems.

3. Compliance with legal and regulatory requirements, and with ethical codes.

4. The quality, performance, and independence of internal and external auditors.

In addition, the audit committee is responsible for the following:

1. Reviewing its own performance against its charter and making recommendations to the board for improving the charter.

2. Retaining and terminating the independent auditors.

3. Implementing a dependable whistleblowing procedure.

4. Addressing any material violations of a code of conduct identified by internal or external auditors or whistleblowers.

5. Discussing corporate disclosures with the management.

6. Reviewing all related party transactions.

7. Periodically reviewing the performance of, and succession planning for, internal and external auditors and key individuals for internal controls.

8. Conducting separate in-camera sessions with the management, and with internal and external auditors.

9. Establishing and reviewing the corporate disclosure policy.

10. Establishing and reviewing the insider trading policy.

11. Establishing and reviewing the code of ethical conduct.

Some areas are particularly sensitive and require special attention by the audit committee.

Issues to be Watched by the Audit Committee

- Provisioning for accounts receivables.
- Valuation of inventories.
- Impairment of goodwill or corporate asset values.
- Aggressive revenue recognition practices.
- Capitalized expenses.
- Underfunded defined employee benefit plans.
- Costs of health and safety plans.
- Coverage and costs of insurance plans.
- Currency, interest, and term mismatch risks.
- Special-purpose entities.
- Costs of environmental obligations.

- Changes in tax policies and aggressiveness of tax management.

- Impact of regulatory developments.

- Potential legal liabilities.

- Recurring/non-recurring costs.

- Complex products that may impact the balance sheet and income statements.

- Swaps and barter transactions.

- Off-balance-sheet liabilities such as guarantees or liens.

- Restructuring or post-merger integration charges.

- Cost of new management systems.

- Any changes in the accounting policies or the chart of accounts.

- Security of financial records.

- Reputational risks.

- Value and risks of intellectual capital assets such as brands and patents.

- Internalization of transparency and accountability as a corporate culture.

- Ensuring that performance management evaluations do not hinder the calculated risk-taking required for entrepreneurship and innovation capabilities.

The audit committee needs also to review the adequacy of the resources for the internal and external audit functions and ensure that their work plans provide an adequate coverage of potential risk areas. The cost effectiveness and prioritization of the audit plans are also among the audit committee's responsibilities. The communications from the audit committee need to have a constructive tone. In particular, when evaluating violations identified by audit function, the committee has to be fair to the management as well. In particular, the tendency to have retrospective evaluations focusing on results rather than on the adherence to procedures may have the effect of diminishing the appetite for risk-taking.

In short, in providing board oversight, a constructive tone builds trust. Every decision needs an evaluation of potential risks, and no manager can get them all right. As long as the outcome is not due to failure to implement governance principles, it is an issue not for criticism but for performance evaluation. Excessive skepticism of management may be a hindrance to value creation. Management needs advisors and coaches, not a judge or a jury. However, it is the duty of the board members to pose tough but fair questions, challenge assumptions, and conduct a rigorous diligence where necessary. Therefore, striking the right balance between providing an effective oversight and motivating the management for calculated risk-taking for continuous learning and innovation is an art at which board members should excel.

"RIGHT OVERSIGHT" – SUMMARY

Providing oversight to the management is a key board responsibility. In order to gain the trust of the stakeholders, and in particular the shareholders, the board has to ensure that the management protects and develops corporate assets for value creation. Both efficiency and effectiveness are key tests of performance, and need to be evaluated from multiple perspectives such as the balance between long term and short term, or risk and reward. Therefore, the completeness and comprehensiveness of key performance indicators to be followed is critical in providing oversight. At the same time, assuming a constructive tone in providing oversight is important for the motivation of the management.

Consistency Consistency of management decisions can be tested only against a clearly identified mission and vision. Also, testing for consistency of actions with corporate policies and values requires such policies and values to be explicitly documented and communicated throughout the organization.

Responsibility It is the responsibility of the board members to pose tough but fair questions, challenge assumptions, and maintain a rigorous diligence.

Accountability Everybody in the organization has to be able to document and explain their decisions. Accountability is a culture.

Fairness An effective internal control system provides for fair evaluations of management decisions.

Transparency Transparency and accuracy in corporate disclosures is a key expectation in the oversight function of the board.

Effectiveness   Identification and prioritization of risks, and taking actions before they materialize, improve the effectiveness of the oversight function. A key benefit of oversight is enabling precautionary actions, and hence not finding fault after the fact. Following best practices in oversight before they become mandatory is itself good practice.

Deployment   Internal controls and oversight are as much a management responsibility at all levels as it is a board responsibility to ensure that such systems are effective.

Conclusion

The board is entrusted with the responsibility of providing guidance and oversight to ensure sustainable value creation. While the boards do not manage the corporation, they govern by setting the rules; selecting the management; reviewing and approving key decisions; coaching, evaluating, and rewarding the management; and ensuring that risk management and internal control systems are effective.

The board's success depends on making sound judgments in numerous situations that involve balancing different interests:

- Risk vs. reward.

- Short term vs. long term.

- Effective oversight vs. motivating management.

- Ethical considerations vs. market practices.

- Competing interests of different stakeholders, namely:

  - Shareholders, small and large.

  - Partners.

  - Management.

  - Employees.

  - Suppliers.

  - Dealers.

  - Customers.

  - Industry players.

  - Public administrators.

  - The community at large.

Such success can be achieved on a sustainable basis only if the board behaves as a role model in implementing the CRAFTED principles of governance in its own operations and ensures that the corporation follows these principles in making key decisions.

Therefore, the effectiveness of a board depends, at a minimum, on the way it addresses issues in the following areas:

- Adoption of a strategic planning process.

- Identifying major risk areas (strategy, operations, leadership, partnerships, and reputation), and ensuring that adequate mitigation strategies and systems are implemented.

- Succession planning, including development plans for senior management and monitoring progress, as well as compensation policies to ensure the ability to attract and retain a high-quality management team.

- Communication and disclosure policies toward authorities, investors, analysts, and press.

- Integrity of internal control and management information systems, including the assurance of the independence of the outside auditors and the availability of a fair and independent whistle-blowing process.

- Adoption of a self evaluation process that covers the board's composition, processes, information, behaviors, climate, and culture.

A new proposal, not yet enacted, by the Canadian authorities for overhauling the corporate governance regime in Canada seems to be in line with the general thinking outlined in this book. The proposal calls for performing the following actions:

Actions Proposed by Canadian Securities Regulators

1. *Creating a framework for oversight and accountability:* The respective roles and responsibilities of the board and executive officers should be established.

2. *Structuring the board to add value:* The board should be comprised of directors who will contribute to its effectiveness.

3. *Attracting and retaining effective directors:* A board should have processes to examine its membership to ensure that directors, individually and collectively, have the necessary competencies and other attributes.

4. *Striving continuously to improve the board's performance:* A board should have processes to improve its performance and that of its committees, if any, and individual directors.

5. *Promoting integrity:* The board should actively promote ethical and responsible behavior and decision-making.

6. *Recognizing and manage conflicts of interest:* The board should establish a sound system of oversight and management of actual and potential conflicts of interest.

7. *Recognizing and manage risk:* The board should establish a sound framework of risk oversight and management.

8. *Compensating appropriately:* The board should ensure that the compensation policies align with the best interests of the corporation.

9. *Engaging effectively with shareholders:* The board should endeavor to stay informed of shareholders' views through the shareholders' meeting process as well as through ongoing dialogue. (I personally would suggest that the principle of effective engagement should apply to all key stakeholders.)

Governance is much more than compliance. Governance ratings and rankings are only an inadequate proxy for measuring the effectiveness of governance, because:

- They are focused on easily observable characteristics.

- Their focus is on inputs, not outputs.

- They do not link governance with company performance.

- They do not say anything about learning and development of governance.

- They do not attempt to measure attitudes, behaviors, or the climate of the board.

Therefore, evaluations of board effectiveness should not only cover every area of compliance with statutory requirements on a regular basis, but also focus on behavioral aspects of governance outlined in this book. Reviewing governance ratings and rankings for benchmarking purposes is a good practice, but unless there is a real governance implication one should not be obsessed with them, because they provide only an inadequate proxy for the right behaviors.

The continuous upgrading of governance practices requires an evaluation of the following aspects of governance on a regular basis:

- Do we have the right people?

- Do we have the right team?

- Do we have the right processes?

- Do we have the right culture?

- Do we get up-to-date and relevant information?

- Are we providing the right kind of guidance?

- Are we providing adequate oversight?

- Are we reviewing our business results and other benchmarks so as to continually improve our performance?

In performing such an evaluation, the board has to regularly assess their own effectiveness in ensuring sustainable improvements in corporate valuations by providing strategic guidance and oversight over management decisions, as well as selecting, developing, and rewarding the management and changing it whenever necessary.[1]

In short, good corporate governance creates a climate and culture where not only the board itself and the top management, but also everybody within the organization, deploys the governance principles of consistency, responsibility, accountability, fairness, transparency, and effectiveness, with discipline in their attitudes, behaviors, and decisions.

NOTE

1 Such a tool is developed by ARGE Consulting. See *ARGE Kurumsal Yönetişm Modeli* (ARGE Corporate Governance Model), 2007.

Suggested Reading

ABA Coordinating Committee on Nonprofit Governance, *Guide to Nonprofit Corporate Governance in the Wake of Sarbanes-Oxley*, American Bar Association, ISBN-10: 1590315677, 25 February 2006.

Aglietta, Michel, Antoine Reberioux, and Antoine Rebzrioux, *Corporate Governance Adrift: A Critique Of Shareholder Value* (Saint-Gobain Centre for Economic Studies), Edward Elgar, ISBN-10: 1845421388, 5 June 2005.

Ali, Paul and Greg N. Gregoriou, *International Corporate Governance After Sarbanes-Oxley*, Wiley Finance Series, Wiley, ISBN-10: 0471775924, 3 March 2006.

Alkhafaji, Abbass F., *A Stakeholder Approach to Corporate Governance: Managing in a Dynamic Environment*, Quorum Books, ISBN-10: 0899304478, 26 September 1989.

All India Management Association, *Corporate Governance and Business Ethics*, Excel Books, ISBN-10: 8174460977, 1 August 2002.

Argüden, Yılmaz, Pınar Ilgaz, and Burak Erşahin, *ARGE Kurumsal Yönetişim Modeli*, ARGE Yayınları, 2007.

Arora, Ramesh K., and Tanjul Saxena, *Corporate Governance*, Jaipur: Mangal Deep, ISBN-10: 8175941561, 27 May 2006.

Arya, P.P., B.B. Tandon, and A.K. Vashit, *Corporate Governance*, Deep & Deep, ISBN-10: 8176294713, 30 October 2004.

Association of Certified Fraud Examiners, *What's A Director to Do?*

Bart, Chris, *20 Questions Directors Should Ask About Strategy*, Canadian Institute of Chartered Accountants, 2006.

Baucus, Max, *Corporate Governance and Executive Compensation: Hearing Before the Committee on Finance, US Senate*, Diane, ISBN-10: 0756744261, 30 September 2002.

Bavly, Dan A., *Corporate Governance and Accountability: What Role for the Regulator, Director, and Auditor?*, Quorum Books, ISBN-10: 1567202802, 28 February 1999.

Bebchuk, Lucian, "Shareholder Access to the Corporate Ballot", Program on Corporate Governance, Harvard Law School, ISBN-10: 0674016580, 3 January 2005.

Berghe, L. van den, *Corporate Governance in a Globalising World: Convergence or Divergence?: A European Perspective*, 1st edn, Springer, ISBN-10: 1402071582, 31 July 2002.

Bhagat, Sanjai and Richard H. Jefferis, *The Econometrics of Corporate Governance Studies*, new edn, MIT Press, ISBN-10: 0262524384, 1 March 2005.

Bhatia, S.K., *Business Ethics and Corporate Governance*, Delhi: Deep & Deep Publications, ISBN-10: 8176295922, 30 September 2004.

Blair, Margaret M., *Ownership and Control: Rethinking Corporate Governance for the Twenty-First Century*, Brookings Institute, ISBN-10: 0815709471, June 1995.

Blair, Margaret M., *The Deal Decade: What Takeovers and Leveraged Buyouts Mean for Corporate Governance*, Brookings Institute, ISBN-10: 0815709455, January 1993.

Blair, Margaret M., *Wealth Creation and Wealth Sharing: A Colloquium on Corporate Governance and Investments in Human Capital*, Washington, DC: Brookings Institute, ISBN-10: 0815709498, May 1996.

Bobowick, Marla J., Sandra R. Hughes, and Berit M. Lakey, *Transforming Board Structure: Strategies for Committees and Task Forces*, Board Source, ISBN-10: 1586860259, 2003.

Bottomley, Stephen, *The Constitutional Corporation: Rethinking Corporate Governance*, Ashgate, ISBN-10: 0754624188, February 2007.

Brancato, Carolyn Kay, *Institutional Investors and Corporate Governance: Best Practices for Increasing Corporate Value*, Irwin, ISBN-10: 0786305584, September 1996.

Branson, Douglas M., *No Seat at the Table: How Corporate Governance and Law Keep Women Out of the Boardroom*, New York University Press, ISBN-10: 0814799736, 1 December 2006.

Brazelton, Julia K. and Janice L. Ammons, *Enron and Beyond: Technical Analysis of Accounting, Corporate Governance, and Securities Issues*, Commerce Clearing House, ISBN-10: 0808008536, 15 October 2002.

Brountas, Paul P., *Boardroom Excellence: A Common Sense Perspective on Corporate Governance*, Jossey-Bass, ISBN-10: 0787976415, 15 September 2004.

Brown, Harold, Peter C. Browning, Carl E. Bill, and John T. Gardner, *Inside the Minds: The Board of the 21st Century: Leading Directors from Wal-Mart, 3M, Lowes and More on the Evolution of Corporate*, Aspatore Books, ISBN-10: 1587622289, December 2002.

Brown, Jim, *The Imperfect Board Member: Discovering the Seven Disciplines of Governance Excellence*, Jossey-Bass, ISBN-10: 0787986100, 29 September 2006.

Buffett, Warren E., *The Essays of Warren Buffett: Lessons for Corporate America*, 1st rev. edn, Cunningham Group, ISBN-10: 0966446119, 11 April 2001.

Cadbury, Adrian, *Corporate Governance and Chairmanship: A Personal View*, Oxford University Press, ISBN-10: 0195666496, 2003.

Canadian Institute of Chartered Accountants, 2006, *20 Questions Directors Should Ask About IT*.

Canadian Institute of Chartered Accountants, 2006, *20 Questions Directors Should Ask About Management's Discussion and Analysis*.

Canadian Institute of Chartered Accountants, 2006, *20 Questions Directors Should Ask About Privacy*.

Canadian Institute of Chartered Accountants, 2006, 20 Questions Series.

Carey, Dennis C. and Michael Patsalos-Fox, "Shaping Strategy from the Boardroom", *The McKinsey Quarterly*, August 2006.

Carver, John, *Boards That Make a Difference: A New Design for Leadership in Nonprofit and Public Organizations*, 2nd edn, Jossey-Bass, ISBN-10: 0787908118, 28 May 1997.

Carver, John, *CarverGuide: Basic Principles of Policy Governance*, 1st edn, Jossey-Bass, ISBN-10: 0787902969, 14 June 1996.

Carver, John, *CarverGuide: Board Self-Assessment*, 1st edn, Jossey-Bass, ISBN-10: 0787908339, 28 March 1997.

Carver, John, *Reinventing Your Board*, rev. edn, San Jossey-Bass, ISBN-10: 0787981818, 24 February 2006.

Castka, Pavel, Chris Bamber, and John Sharp, *Implementing Effective Corporate Social Responsibility and Corporate Governance: A Framework*, BSI Standards, ISBN-10: 0580439534, 30 September 2004.

Chait, Richard P., *Governance as Leadership: Reframing the Work of Nonprofit Boards*, Wiley, ISBN-10: 0471684201, 22 October 2004.

Chambers, Andrew, *Tottel's Corporate Governance Handbook*, 3rd edn, Tottel, ISBN-10: 1845920821, January 2005.

Chandra, Ramesh and Ritu Aneja, *Corporate Governance for Sustainable Environment*, Gyan, ISBN-10: 8182051053, 30 September 2004.

Charan, Ram, *Boards That Deliver: Advancing Corporate Governance From Compliance to Competitive Advantage*, Jossey-Bass, ISBN-10: 0787971391, 3 February 2005.

Charan, Ram, *Juntas Directivas Que Contribuyen/Boards That Deliver: Del Simple Cumplimiento a la Ventaja Competitiva/Advancing Corporate Governance from Compliance to Competitive Advantage*, trans. edn, Grupo Editorial Norma, ISBN-10: 9580491283, 30 March 2006.

Charkham, Jonathan, John L. Colley, Jacqueline L. Doyle, Wallace Stettinius, and George Logan, *Keeping Better Company: Corporate Governance Ten Years On Corporate Governance*, 2nd edn, Oxford University Press, ISBN-10: 0199243182, 9 December 2005.

Chartered Accountants of Canada, *Beyond Compliance: Building a Governance Culture*.

Chew, Donald H., *Corporate Governance at the Crossroads: A Book of Readings*, 1st edn, McGraw-Hill/Irwin, ISBN-10: 0072957085, 30 January 2004.

Chorafas, Dimitris N., *Fair Value and Corporate Governance: The Impact on Budgets, Balance Sheets and Management Accounts*, Butterworth-Heinemann, ISBN-10: 0750668954, 3 April 2006.

Clark, Gordon L. and Darius Wojcik, *The Geography of Finance: Corporate Governance in a Global Marketplace*, Oxford University Press, ISBN-10: 0199213364, 8 June 2007.

Clarke, Thomas and Marie Dela Rama, *Corporate Governance and Globalization*, 3 vols, Sage, ISBN-10: 1412928990, 27 October 2006.

Clarke, Thomas, *Theories of Corporate Governance: The Theoretical Foundations*, 1st edn, Routledge, ISBN-10: 0415323088, 29 September 2004.

Clemons, Calvin K., *The Perfect Board*, Synergy Books, ISBN-10: 0975592270, 15 September 2005.

Cohen, Stephen S. and Gavin Boyd, *Corporate Governance and Globalization: Long Range Planning Issues*, Edward Elgar, ISBN-10: 184064179, October 2000.

Colley, John L., *Corporate Governance*, 1st edn, McGraw-Hill, ISBN-10: 0071403469, 20 June 2003.

Colley, John L., *What Is Corporate Governance?*, 1st edn, McGraw-Hill, ISBN-10: 007144448-3, 6 December 2004.

Coombes, Paul and Simon Chiu-Yin Wong, "Why Codes of Governance Work", *The McKinsey Quarterly*, part 2, 2004.

Correia da Silva, Luis, Marc Goergen, and Luc Renneboog, *Dividend Policy and Corporate Governance*, Oxford University Press, ISBN-10: 0199259305, 8 April 2004.

Crawford, Curtis J., *Compliance & Conviction: The Evolution of Enlightened Corporate Governance*, XCEO, Inc., ISBN-10: 0976901919, 22 November 2006.

David Hume Institute, *Corporate Governance*, Edinburgh University Press, ISBN-10: 0748608591, 15 April 1996.

Davies, Adrian, *Best Practice in Corporate Governance: Building Reputation And Sustainable Success*, Gower, ISBN-10: 0566086441, 31 January 2006.

Davis, Ian, "What is the Business of Business?", *The McKinsey Quarterly*, August 2005.

Dess, Gregory G. and G.T. (Tom) Lumpkin, *Strategic Management with Corporate Governance Update and PowerWeb*, 1st edn, McGraw-Hill/Irwin, ISBN-10: 0072872292, 4 December 2002.

Dietl, Helmut M., *Capital Markets and Corporate Governance in Japan, Germany and the United States: Organizational Response to Market Inefficiencies*, 1st edn, TF-ROUTL, ISBN-10: 0415171881, 18 December 1997.

Dimma, William A., *Tougher Boards for Tougher Times: Corporate Governance in the Post-Enron Era*, Wiley, ISBN-10: 0470837306, 10 March 2006.

Dimsdale, Nicholas and Martha Prevezer, *Capital Markets and Corporate Governance*, Oxford University Press, ISBN-10: 0198287887, 7 June 1994.

Dunphy, Dexter and Suzanne Benn, *Corporate Governance and Sustainability: Challenges for Theory and Practice*, 1st edn, Routledge, ISBN-10: 0415380634, August 2006.

Ernst & Young LLP, Peter Wallace, and John Zinkin, *Corporate Governance*, Wiley, ISBN-10: 0470821124, 1 February 2005.

Ernst & Young, *Non-Executive Directors and Their Contribution to Business Performance*, 2004.

Ezzamel, Mahmoud, *Governance, Directors and Boards*, Edward Elgar, ISBN-10: 1845421035, 5 June 2005.

Federowicz, Michał and Ruth Aguilera, *Corporate Governance in a Changing Economic and Political Environment: Trajectories of Institutional Change*, Palgrave Macmillan, ISBN-10: 1403920761, 3 April 2004.

Felton, Robert F. and Mark Watson, "Change Across the Board, " *The McKinsey Quarterly*, November 2002.

Felton, Robert F. and Pamela Keenan Fritz, "The View from the Boardroom," *The McKinsey Quarterly*, March 2005.

Felton, Robert F. and Simon C. Y. Wong, "How to Separate the Roles of Chairman and CEO," *The McKinsey Quarterly*, November 2004.

Felton, Robert F., Alec Hudnut, and Jennifer Van Heeckeren, "Putting a Value on Board Governance," *The McKinsey Quarterly*, November 1996.

Felton, Robert F., Alec Hudnut, and Valda Witt, "Building a Stronger Board," *The McKinsey Quarterly*, May 1995.

Filatotchev, Igor and Mike Wright, *The Life Cycle of Corporate Governance*, Edward Elgar, ISBN-10: 1845422147, 5 August 2005.

Fraser, John and Hugh Lindsay, *20 Questions Directors Should Ask About Internal Audit*, Canadian Institute of Chartered Accountants, 2006.

Fukao, Mitsuhiro, *Financial Integration, Corporate Governance, and the Performance of Multinational Companies*, Brookings Institute, ISBN-10: 081572988X, June 1995.

Garratt, Bob, *Thin on Top: Why Corporate Governance Matters and How to Measure and Improve Board Performance*, 2nd rev. edn, Nicholas Brealey, ISBN-10: 1857883241, 8 November 2006.

Goergen, Marc, *Corporate Governance and Financial Performance: A Study of German and UK Initial Public Offerings*, Edward Elgar, ISBN-10: 1858989787, January 1999.

Gourevitch, Peter A., *Political Power and Corporate Control: The New Global Politics of Corporate Governance*, Princeton University Press, ISBN-10: 0691133816, 1 August 2007.

Grandori, Anna, *Corporate Governance and Firm Organization: Microfoundations and Structural Forms*, new edn, Oxford University Press, ISBN-10: 0199286795, 2 February 2006.

Green, Scott, *Sarbanes-Oxley and the Board of Directors: Techniques and Best Practices for Corporate Governance*, Wiley, ISBN-10: 0471736082, 2005.

Greville, Elizabeth, David Crawford, *20 Questions Directors Should Ask About Director Compensation*, Canadian Institute of Chartered Accountants, 2006.

Greville, Elizabeth and David Crawford, *20 Questions Directors Should Ask About Executive Compensation*, Canadian Institute of Chartered Accountants, 2006.

Gugler, Klaus, *Corporate Governance and Economic Performance*, Oxford University Press, ISBN-10: 0199245703, 31 August 2001.

Haazen, Walter, *Corporate Governance: So What?*, Trafford, ISBN-10: 1412202000, 10 November 2006.

Hamilton, Stewart, *Is Your Company at Risk?*, http://www.imd.ch/research/challenges/TC010-06.cfm

Hardesty, David E., *Practical Guide to Corporate Governance and Accounting: Implementing the Requirements of the Sarbanes-Oxley Act*, 2005 edn, ISBN-10: 0791355241, December 2004.

Hilb, Martin, *New Corporate Governance: Successful Board Management Tools*, 2nd edn, Springer, ISBN-10: 3540281673, 11 May 2006.

Houston, Bill and Nigel Lewis, *The Independent Director: Handbook and Guide to Corporate Governance*, Butterworth-Heinemann, ISBN-10: 0750606592, August 1992.

Huse, Morten, *Boards, Governance and Value Creation: The Human Side of Corporate Governance*, Cambridge University Press, ISBN-10: 0521606349, 14 May 2007.

Hutchinson, Allan C., *The Companies We Keep: Corporate Governance for a Democratic Society*, Irwin Law, ISBN-10: 1552211169, January 2006.

Jensen, Michael C. and Joe Fuller, *How Bigger Dividends Build Trust*, Financial Times, 6 October, 2003.

Junarso, Tri, *Comprehensive Approach To Corporate Governance*, iUniverse, ISBN-10: 0595401600, 21 September 2006.

Kaen, Fred R., *A Blueprint for Corporate Governance: Strategy, Accountability, and the Preservation of Shareholder Value*, 1st edn, AMACOM/American Management Association, ISBN-10: 081440586X, February 2003.

Karpoff, Jonathan M., M. Wayne Marr Jr, and Morris G. Danielson, *Corporate Governance and Firm Performance*, Research Foundation of AIMR & Blackwell, ISBN-10: 094320528X, 6 November 2000.

Keasey, Kevin, Steve Thompson, and Michael Wright, *Corporate Governance: Accountability, Enterprise and International Comparisons*, Wiley, ISBN-10: 0470870303, 27 May 2005.

Keasey, Kevin, Steve Thompson, and Mike Wright, *Corporate Governance: Economic and Financial Issues*, new edn, Oxford University Press, ISBN-10: 019828991X, 16 September 1997.

Kim, Kenneth A., *Corporate Governance*, 2nd edn, Prentice Hall, ISBN-10: 0131735349, 23 March 2006.

Kleinschmidt, Maik, *Venture Capital, Corporate Governance, and Firm Value*, Deutscher Universitäts-Verlag, ISBN-10: 3835007181, 1 March 2007.

Kocourek, Paul F., Christian Burger, and Bill Birchard, *Corporate Governance: Hard Facts about Soft Behaviors*, http://www.strategy-business.com/press/16635507/8322

Korn/Ferry, *33rd Quarterly Board of Directors Study*.

Lazonick, William and Mary O'Sullivan, *Corporate Governance and Sustainable Prosperity (Jerome Levy Economics Institute)*, Palgrave Macmillan, ISBN-10: 0333777573, 12 January 2002.

Leblanc, Richard and James Gillies, *Inside the Boardroom: How Boards Really Work and the Coming Revolution in Corporate Governance*, Wiley, ISBN-10: 0470835206, 8 June 2005.

Leblanc, Richard W., *20 Questions Directors Should Ask About Governance Assessments*, Canadian Institute of Chartered Accountants, 2006.

Ledgerwood, Grant, *Greening the Boardroom: Corporate Governance and Business Sustainability*, Greenleaf, ISBN-10: 1874719020, September 1997.

Lee, Thomas A., *Financial Reporting and Corporate Governance*, Wiley, ISBN-10: 0470026812, 16 January 2007.

Leslie, Keith, Mark A. Loch, and William Schaninger, "Managing Your Organization by the Evidence", *The McKinsey Quarterly*, August 2006.

Lindsay, Hugh, *20 Questions Directors Should Ask About Building a Board*, Canadian Institute of Chartered Accountants, 2006.

Lindsay, Hugh, *20 Questions Directors Should Ask About Risk*, Canadian Institute of Chartered Accountants, 2006.

Lipman, Frederick D., *Corporate Governance Best Practices: Strategies for Public, Private, and Not-for-Profit Organizations*, Wiley, ISBN-10: 0470043792, 1 September 2006.

Lorsch, Jay W. and Rakesh Khurana, "Changing Leaders: The Board's Role in CEO Succession", *Harvard Business Review*, May 1999, 99308.

Lovallo, Dan P. and Olivier Sibony, "Distortions and Deceptions in Strategic Decisions", *The McKinsey Quarterly*, February 2006.

Lowy, Martin, *Corporate Governance for Public Company Directors*, Aspen, ISBN-10: 0735541035, 1 February 2003.

Luo, Yadong, *Global Dimensions of Corporate Governance: Global Dimensions of Business*, Blackwell, ISBN 9781405137072, 5 September 2006.

Maclean, Mairi, Charles Harvey, and Jon Press, *Business Elites and Corporate Governance in France and the UK (French Politics, Society and Culture)*, Palgrave Macmillan, ISBN-10: 1403935793, 2 March 2006.

Mak, Yuen Teen, *From Conformance to Performance: Best Corporate Governance Practices for Asian Companies*, McGraw-Hill Education (Asia), ISBN-10: 0071247815, 14 July 2005.

Malik, Fredmund, *Effective Top Management: Beyond the Failure of Corporate Governance and Shareholder Value*, Wiley, ISBN-10: 3527501177, 13 June 2006.

Mallin, Christine A., *Handbook on International Corporate Governance*, Edward Elgar, ISBN-10: 1845420349, 30 October 2006.

Mallin, Christine, *International Corporate Governance: A Case Study Approach*, Edward Elgar, ISBN-10: 1845420357, 6 May 2006.

Mäntysaari, Petri, *Comparative Corporate Governance: Shareholders as a Rule-maker*, 1st edn, Springer, ISBN-10: 3540253807, 22 July 2005.

Maw, Nigel Graham and Alison Alsbury, *Maw on Corporate Governance*, Brookfield Vermont, ISBN-10: 1855213788, June 1994.

McCahery, Joseph, Piet Moerland, Theo Raaijmakers, and Luc Renneboog, *Corporate Governance Regimes: Convergence and Diversity*, Oxford University Press, ISBN-10: 0199247870, 7 November 2002.

McGregor, Lynn, *The Human Face of Corporate Governance*, Palgrave Macmillan, ISBN-10: 0333772059, 8 December 2000.

McKinsey & Company, *Global Investor Opinion Survey: Key Findings*, July 2002.

Millstein, Ira, *The Recurrent Crisis in Corporate Governance*, 1st edn, Stanford Business Books, ISBN-10: 0804750866, 18 August 2004.

Monks, Robert A.G. and Nell Minow, *Watching the Watchers: Corporate Governance for the 21st Century*, Blackwell, ISBN-10: 1557868662, May 1996.

Monks, Robert A.G., *Corporate Governance*, 3rd edn, Blackwell, ISBN-10: 1405116986, 1 December 2003.

Montgomery, Cynthia A. and Rhonda Kaufman, "The Board's Missing Link, " *Harvard Business Review*, March 2003.

Mullerat, Ramon and Daniel Brennan, *Corporate Social Responsibility: The Corporate Governance of the 21st Century*, Kluwer Law, ISBN-10: 9041123245, 30 January 2005.

Murray, Alan, *Revolt in the Boardroom: The New Rules of Power in Corporate America*, 1st edn, Collins, ISBN-10: 0060882476, 8 May 2007.

Nadler, David A., *Building Better Boards: A Blueprint for Effective Governance*, Jossey-Bass, ISBN-10: 078798180X, 30 December 2005.

Naidoo, Ramani and Selby Baqwa, *Corporate Governance*, Double Storey, ISBN-10: 1919930086, 5 April 2007.

Nelson, Brian, *Law and Ethics in Global Business Integrating Corporate Governance into Business Decisions*, 1st edn, Routledge, ISBN-10: 041537779X, 13 January 2006.

Newquist, Scott, Max Russell, and John C. Bogle, *Putting Investors First: Real Solutions for Better Corporate Governance*, 1st edn, Bloomberg, ISBN-10: 1576601412, August 2003.

O'Brien, Justin, *Governing the Corporation: Regulation and Corporate Governance in an Age of Scandal and Global Markets*, Wiley, ISBN-10: 0470015063, 23 September 2005.

Organisation for Economic Co-operation & Development, *Corporate Governance of State-Owned Enterprises: A Survey Of OECD Countries*, ISBN-10: 9264009426, 30 June 2005, www.oecd.org

Organization for Economic Cooperation & Development, *Corporate Governance In Asia: A Comparative Perspective (Emerging Economies Transition)*, ISBN-10: 9264183280, December 2004.

Osano, Hiroshi and Toshiaki Tachibanaki, *Banking, Capital Markets and Corporate Governance*, Palgrave Macmillan, ISBN-10: 0333771362, 12 January 2002.

O'Sullivan, Mary, *Contests for Corporate Control: Corporate Governance and Economic Performance in the United States and Germany*, Oxford University Press, new edn, ISBN-10: 0199244863, 6 August 2001.

Owen, Geoffrey, Tom Kirchmaier, and Jeremy Grant, *Corporate Governance in the US and Europe: Where Are We Now?*, Palgrave Macmillan, ISBN-10: 1403998663, 16 February 2006.

Plessis, Jean du, James McConvill, and Mirko Bagaric, *Principles of Contemporary Corporate Governance*, Cambridge University Press, ISBN-10: 0521617839, 24 October 2005.

Prentice, D.D. and P.R.J. Holland, *Contemporary Issues in Corporate Governance*, Oxford University Press, ISBN-10: 0198258593, 11 September 1993.

Roche, Julian, *Corporate Governance in Asia*, 1st edn, Routledge, ISBN-10: 0415339766, 19 May 2005.

Rossouw, G. J. Deon, and Alejo Jose G. Sison, *Global Perspectives on Ethics of Corporate Governance*, Palgrave Macmillan, ISBN-10: 1403975841, 28 November 2006.

Roth, James and Donald Espersen, *Internal Audit's Role in Corporate Governance: Sarbanes-Oxley Compliance*, Spi Pap/CD edn, Institute of Internal Auditors Research Foundation, ISBN-10: 0894135104, June 2003.

Rubinstein, Saul A. and Thomas A. Kochan, *Learning from Saturn: Possibilities for Corporate Governance and Employee Relations (ILR Press Books)*, 1st rev. edn, Cunningham, ISBN-10: 0966446119, 11 April 2001.

Salmon, Walter J., *Harvard Business Review on Corporate Governance (Harvard Business Review Paperback Series)*, Harvard Business School Press, ISBN-10: 1578512379, January 2000.

Sherman, Hugh and Rajeswararao Chaganti, *Corporate Governance and the Timeliness of Change: Reorientation in 100 American Firms*, Quorum, ISBN-10: 1567200877, 30 August 1998.

Singh, Devi and Subhash Garg, *Corporate Governance*, Excel, ISBN-10: 817446252X, 1 August 2002.

Skousen, K. Fred, Steven Glover, and Douglas Prawitt, *Introduction to the SEC and Corporate Governance*, 1st edn, South-Western College Publishing, ISBN-10: 0324226985, 2 August 2004.

Slywotzky, Adrian J., *The Upside: The 7 Stratetegies for Turning Big Threats into Growth Breakthroughs*, Crown Business ISBN 978-0-307-35101-2, 2007.

Sonnenfeld, Jeffrey A., "What Makes Great Boards Great", *Harvard Business Review*, 1 September 2002.

Sonnenfeld, Jeffrey, "Good Governance and the Misleading Myths of Bad Metrics", *Academy of Management Executive*, vol. 18, no.1, 2004.

Spira, Laura F., *The Audit Committee: Performing Corporate Governance*, 1st edn, Springer, ISBN-10: 0792376498, 1 January 2002.

Steinberg, Richard M., *Corporate Governance and the Board: What Works Best*, Institute of Internal Auditors Research Foundation, ISBN-10: 0894134388, 1 May 2000.

Thevenoz, Luc and Rashid Bahar, *Conflicts of Interest: Corporate Governance and Financial Markets*, Kluwer Law, ISBN-10: 9041125787, 5 February 2007.

United Nations Conference on Trade and Development, *Guidance on Good Practices in Corporate Governance Disclosure*, United Nations, ISBN-10: 9211127041, 25 August 2006.

Vinella, Peter and Jeanette Jin, *Corporate Governance and Operational Risk A Practical Guide (Wiley Finance)*, Wiley, ISBN-10: 0471707023, 3 May 2006.

Vives, Xavier, *Corporate Governance: Theoretical and Empirical Perspectives*, new edn, Cambridge University Press, ISBN-10: 0521032032, 23 November 2006.

Warren, Richard C., *Corporate Governance and Accountability*, Liverpool Academic Press, ISBN-10: 190349902X, 30 November 2000.

Waterson, Michael, *Competition, Monopoly and Corporate Governance: Essays in Honour of Keith Cowling*, Edward Elgar, ISBN-10: 1843760894, December 2003.

Wearing, Robert T., *Cases in Corporate Governance*, Sage, ISBN-10: 1412908779, 24 May 2005.

Wong, Simon C.Y. and Dominic Barton, "Improving Board Performance in Emerging Markets", *The McKinsey Quarterly*, 2006. Febuary

Index